ARNOLDUS NOACH
BIOGRAFIE VAN EEN VRIEND

ARNOLD NOACH
BIOGRAPHY OF A FRIEND

Arnold Noach

ARNOLDUS NOACH
BIOGRAFIE VAN EEN VRIEND

ARNOLD NOACH
BIOGRAPHY OF A FRIEND

by
Scotford Lawrence

Arnold Noach: Biography of a Friend
Scotford Lawrence

Published by Aspect Design 2020
Malvern, Worcestershire, United Kingdom.

Designed and Printed by Aspect Design
89 Newtown Road, Malvern, Worcs. WR14 1PD
United Kingdom
Tel: 01684 561567
E-mail: books@aspect-design.net
Website: www.aspect-design.net

Typeset in Adobe Garamond Pro

ISBN 978-1-912078-20-2

CONTENTS

ACKNOWLEDGEMENTS

A large number of people have helped me in writing this biography. The most important have been those few who actually knew Arnold Noach or who have provided documents, reminiscences, and remembered fragments, all of which have gone to build up the life and character of my subject. There have also been many others in academic and official positions who have also made useful contributions. I would like to thank them all and say that, without their help and generosity, this biography could not have been written.

Francine Albach Amsterdam
Esther Boeles University of Amsterdam
Edward Brand Oswestry
John and Bronwen Brindley Ripon, Yorkshire
Marleen Christensen-Michel University of Amsterdam
Martin Clayton The Royal Collections, Windsor
Paul Hellmann Rotterdam
Jill Hughes Aubourn Lincoln
Anton Kras Jewish Cultural Centre Amsterdam
Julian Lawrence Brighton
Ruud Lindeman Museum of the Resistance, Amsterdam
Angela Mazairac Chancellery of Orders of the Netherlands, Den Haag
Griselda Pollock Leeds
Adrian Rifkin London
Ruth Rosen London
Philip and Wendy Sutcliffe Edinburgh
Jennifer Stead Leeds
Peter Tomson De Oude Kerk, Amsterdam
Jenö Toppler Wassenaar, Netherlands
Henk Visée Amsterdam
Sophie Rose Williams London

1

INTRODUCTION

This short biography of a family friend is written to bring together a mass of disparate information about the life of Arnold Noach and to try and assemble a coherent story of his life, from his birth in Amsterdam in 1910 until his death in London in 1976 at the age of only sixty-six. One of the main purposes is to provide for Arnold's godson, my son Julian Lawrence and for my grandchildren, a description of this most unusual, immensely knowledgeable, but at the same time jolly, humorous man whom Julian was only able to know up to the age of twelve.

Arnold died shortly after his retirement as emeritus professor of art history at the University of Leeds. When a friend, professor Reg 'Spanish' Brown, was asked to write an appreciation on Arnold's retirement for the University Journal, he turned to the former secretary of the department of fine art, Margaret Lawrence, for help. What they soon found out was that, although there were a number of key dates and points in Arnold's life that could easily be established, there were also many 'gaps' and periods when no-one could say where he was or how he was occupied. His life appeared to have been peculiarly compartmentalized with gaps in between those times which could not be readily accounted for. He was, to a remarkable extent, a man of mystery.

It has been my task in compiling this biography to try to fill in those gaps and to produce a complete story of who he was, what he did, most particularly, his life before and during World War 2, when he had to go into hiding and lived as a fugitive in his own country for several years. While it has been comparatively easy to reconstruct Arnold's life from his arrival in England in 1946, finding out about and reconstructing his life in Amsterdam pre-war and during the war years has been, understandably, much more difficult. But I have been enormously helped by contacts in the Netherlands who have been free with their own assembled information and have also helped me with contacts and leads to other people and so on. I have been given access to notes, personal writings and copies of Arnold's own letters which have proved invaluable. I am truly grateful to all of these helpers as also to various people in official positions in Holland and in England who have looked up and searched out official records which have given me further 'pegs' on which to hang this biographical story.

The number of people who knew Arnold personally is now only a small and diminishing number and there is therefore an urgency for me to obtain from them as much information as they are able to give. But what I have received, apart from the solid basic information which I was seeking, has been a mass of amusing and entertaining stories of curious mishaps, adventures and simply funny incidents which also serve to flesh out the image of a man who might otherwise appear only as a rather severe academic. Arnold was fun to know. At the time he came into my own life in the 1950s, he was a dapper, always formally dressed, small man, slightly tubby, bald headed and clean-shaven who carried about him a *bon vivant* atmosphere of cologne and good cigars. He had a ready smile but his face in repose would lapse into a distant severity which might have been an outward reflection of the life through which he had passed and which he had miraculously survived. It was very much the face of a Dutch burger and could have easily graced a black-clad and starch-ruffed assembly in a group portrait in the Rijksmuseum.

I want to reflect all of these aspects of a man who was known mainly as an art historian, and as an extremely charismatic lecturer and a good student mentor. But, in one important area, he failed himself, in that he only ever wrote one major work on his subject. He did not get down in writing so much of the encyclopædic knowledge of European art and architecture which he knew so intimately and so thoroughly. This was a great pity and a serious shortcoming which detracted from his reputation as a scholar and deprived him of the recognition which he might otherwise have enjoyed and which he certainly deserved. I will try to identify the reasons for this as we look at the story of his life and how this reflected on his career and his achievements.

Arnold was also a family man and an immensely proud and loving father who lived happily with his wife, the Austrian psychiatrist, Ilse Hellmann, whom he married when he was already thirty-nine years old and she was a couple of years his senior. He doted on his daughter Margaret (Maggie) who went on to a successful career as a literary agent, most particularly for children's books. And I have fond memories of their tall rambling house in Chelsea where the walls were lined with fascinating artworks, most particularly historical prints of Continental architecture. All of this I hope to be able to reflect in the life story of a most interesting, intriguing and enigmatic man of whom I have the fondest memories.

I am writing this memoire from a mass of information which has been kindly supplied by the many people who have helped me. In using this information, I will not reference it every time within my writing as one would do for an academic work. There will be no, 'Dr. 'x' said that....' or 'Mr. 'y' mentions that....' or inserted numbers indicating notes at the end of each chapter. I will use the information as given to me, having checked, where I can, that it is accurate, but of course we are now relying on memories of more than seventy years ago, so there is an understandable risk of error and of 'colouring' that information with one's own view of it. I make no excuses for this. This is, after all, a personal memory of a dear friend and that alone colours what I write and the way I write it.

Please note that this biography is written about a man who, in Dutch, was named Arnoldus Noach. To me and his contemporaries in England, he was 'Arnold,' while within his family and close friends who had known him from his early years in the Netherlands, he was 'Nol' and to his family, even as 'Nolletje' (Little Nol). Any of these forms of his name will be used in the text as appropriate.

2

EARLY HOME LIFE
AMSTERDAM

Arnoldus Noach was born on 9 December 1910, the second child of Meijer Noach and his wife Judith Noach-Boom. They already had a daughter, Julia, some five years older than Arnold.

Meijer Noach was a jeweller who had a shop in the central Amstelstraat, but the family home was at Valeriusstraat 63, in Amsterdam Zuid. This was a large, spacious terrace town house. Much of Valeriusstraat has recently been redeveloped and, while there is still a number sixty-three, it is a modern house occupying the same site. The Noachs also owned several other properties around the city and elsewhere in the Netherlands and were comfortably prosperous Amsterdam bourgeoisie. They were Jewish, but non-observant and secular.

Arnold's sister Julia later said that, prior to his birth, she had found her parents very cold toward her and, in her own words, she lived in an 'ice desert.' Perhaps her mother was not of an affectionate nature but Julia was very happy at the birth of her younger brother and she remained devoted to him and possessive of him throughout their lives. In fact, when Arnold married in 1949, his wife Ilse, felt a certain friction in that Julia still wanted to fuss over Arnold and 'look after' him, even as a married man.

The parents had high expectations of their children and Julia, who showed a considerable musical talent, went on to become a concert pianist before 1939 but ceased at the outbreak of war

Meijer Noach, Arnold's father

and never resumed her musical career afterwards, although in a letter written by Arnold to Julia in the summer of 1945, he writes of arranging to get back Julia's piano which, apparently had been given for safety to someone else away from Amsterdam. Similarly, Arnold was encouraged in his academic studies and on 28 September 1928 he enrolled at the University of Amsterdam, at first to study architecture, very soon changing to art history but continuing with a special emphasis on the history of architecture. From a first degree, he went on to carry out research and write and present his doctoral thesis, for which he was examined (a public viva) on 22 June 1937.

The university also offered other opportunities in Arnold's student life. Here he made contact with a group of smart friends and they became a 'set' who remained in contact after the first degree stage and went on to become pivotal during the later vicissitudes of the war years. Most important amongst these friends was Ben Albach, and his older brother Jan, whom Arnold may first have met at the student theatre of the University. He first met Ben in 1930 and they became close friends, with Arnold's activities in art history and architecture fitting in well with Ben's lifelong interest and research into the Dutch theatre and into its history. But while

Arnold in his twenties

Arnold was in the fortunate position of being able to carry on with his research without any financial constraints, Ben could not afford this luxury and this did produce some friction between them. Ben loved the theatre and had even managed to perform in plays locally. In 1929 he had played in a Dutch performance of a Noel Coward play, which in its translated language was titled 'Weekend,' but in English is Noel Coward's famous play, 'Hay Fever.'

Arnold and Ben did everything together, going off to visit art exhibitions and getting invitations to see the famous, privately owned art collections of Bosch Reitz and Frank Luns. In 1936 they made a trip to Vienna together to further Arnold's interest and knowledge of architecture.

Arnold also made his way to Italy during the inter-war years and developed a life-long love for that country, its culture, its art and its architecture. As professor of art history at Leeds University three decades later, he conducted study parties to Italy where his encyclopædic knowledge and his boundless enthusiasm for his subject were clearly in evidence. He spent a long time studying the architecture of Venice and even had an office in the Doge's palace made available to him from which to carry out his work there. There was however, one incident to which Arnold referred much later when he was set upon by a group of Italian *fascisti* and roughed up, but Arnold did not give any details of exactly what happened, though this may have been just another case of their general xenophobia.

Back home in the Netherlands, Ben and Arnold managed to obtain access to the basement storage of the Stadsschouwburg, the City of Amsterdam Civic Theatre, where they found records and documents of plays and stage settings going back three and a half centuries. In 1934, they helped to arrange an exhibition of 350 years of the theatre from this material and this became and remained Ben's main area of academic interest throughout his life. During this time Ben had even been preparing set designs for major theatrical productions for plays commemorating events in the history of the city. Arnold and Ben became inseparable and this was sufficiently obvious that Ben's brother Jan was actually moved to warn their parents of the possibility that this was becoming a homosexual relationship, though there was never any outward suggestion of this from the behaviour of Arnold.

Arnold was awarded his doctorate in 1937 (D.Litt. and Phil.) for his thesis on the architectural development of the Oude Kerk, Amsterdam's main church and the oldest surviving building in the city. He had taken a leisurely nine years from his first arrival at the university until the completion and acceptance of his doctorate. This was an occasion for rejoicing and a formal celebration dinner for fourteen guests held at the

De Oude Kerk, Amsterdam today

Paviljeon Apollo restaurant situated overlooking a canal in the city centre. Both the Noach and Albach families were present together with a number of guests from among family friends and Arnold's university friends.

Arnold's developed his doctoral thesis into a book, 'De Oude Kerk te Amsterdam Biografie van een Gebouw' published by Den Noord-Hollandsch Uitgevers Maatschschappij in 1939. It is a substantial volume of nearly 300 pages with both diagrammatic and plan images and photographs of the building and of images of the building taken from earlier documents. Typical of its period, it does not have, as almost all books now have, a colophon giving biographical information about the author, and technical data on the illustrators, design, typefaces and all the other details which the modern reader might wish to know. It is even more surprising to find that there is no acknowledgment in the text of others who helped in the production of the final work – no thanks to the photographer or illustrator or those who prepared and drew the various plans and drawings. In fact, all of that work had been done for Arnold by Ben Albach for the drawings and Jan for the photographs. Jan was a keen amateur photographer and, while he now worked for a city centre shipping company, the three of them would 'bunk off' from Jan's office to Arnold's project during lunch breaks and do their research, drawing and photography. Understandably, the fact that there was no acknowledgment or thanks in Arnold's final work rather hurt the Albach brothers.

Arnold loved his native city, its structure, its idiosyncrasies and its curious interface of high culture and art with the rough-and-ready seaport

De Oude Kerk. The book of Arnold Noach's doctoral thesis

atmosphere of its waterways and its suggestion of seafaring and the great Dutch mercantile tradition, accessible at every street end. Indeed, he claimed that the whole of the Dutch character was exemplified by an exchange which he heard as a young man as two barges, steered by the notoriously coarse-tongued barge-women, jockeyed for a place in one of the city's locks. Their boat handling degenerated into a mutual slanging match. One shouted across at the other who was visibly pregnant, "I 'ope you gets a brass bastard, then you'll 'ave to polish the bugger!" Arnold claimed that however depraved a Dutch woman was, she would still feel compelled to polish anything made of brass which she possessed! This was inherent in the Dutch character.

Another of the city's 'free entertainments' was the almost weekly occurrence of the police or city authorities having to drag cars out of the canals as a result of drivers' carelessness, failure to put on the parking brake or simply misjudging their driving.

Arnold claimed that the city's newspapers kept the headline, *'Auto gesleept uit Kanaal'* (car dragged from canal) permanently set up in type.

While Ben Albach pursued his interest in the theatre and stage design, Arnold himself was also considering a job. The post of professor of art history at the University of Amsterdam had become vacant and Arnold applied for but did not get the job, which went to the older and more experienced J. Q. Van Regteren Altena (1899-1980) who was already a well-known art historian and collector and whose drawing collection was donated after his death to the Rijksmuseum of which he had been a director. Apart from the difference in age and experience, there was also the suggestion that there might have been a degree of anti-Semitism in the choice, though there is no firm evidence to support this.

At this time in 1939, we do know that Arnold acted as Master of Ceremonies at the celebrations of the wedding of his childhood friend Tetta Soesman with the journalist Arthur Wijngaard, held in the New Synagogue. (now the Jewish Historical Museum) in Amsterdam.

Arnold's was a life of comfortable, prosperous, leisurely post-graduate art historical research, carried out without the usual financial constraints and enjoyed amongst a set of friends in the smart metropolitan society of an important city of European culture. On 1 September 1939, when Arnold was twenty-nine years old, the Second World War broke out.

3

WAR

During the First World War (1914-1918), Holland had declared neutrality and they managed to maintain this position throughout the whole four year period when slaughter and devastation was happening just beyond their borders in Belgium and in France. To some extent, this was because the Germans recognized that having Holland undisturbed by war was beneficial to them, since they were important suppliers of goods, food and engineering products upon which Germany relied. Since the Dutch aeronautical engineer Anthony Fokker had chosen to set up his aeroplane company in Germany in 1912, and his firm became a major supplier of military aircraft to the Germans, there remained a strong wish not to alienate the Dutch during the war.

Also strategically, the river Rhine, a major artery of German commerce and supply, flowed out to the sea through the Netherlands and, quite understandably, Germany did not want that area to become a battle ground if this could be avoided by respecting Dutch neutrality.

As the war intensified, there was a large influx of Belgian refugees into Holland. Queen Wilhelmina established a charity to which Dutch children were asked to donate toys for the refugee children. Arnold used to say that he remembered certain of his toys being taken 'to give to the poor Belgian children'.....and as a child, he resented it!

When Nazi Germany became increasingly dominant and aggressive during the 1930s, Jews in many European countries thought that Holland could provide a possible refuge for them. There was a growing influx of Jewish refugees into Holland in the latter half of the 1930s and particularly after the *Anschluß*, the takeover by Germany of Austria in 1938.

In 1939 the Dutch government established a transit camp at Westerbork in eastern Holland for arriving Jewish refugees who were housed there in comfortable conditions before they could move on into the general community. It is the cruellest of ironies that the camp at Westerbork was, during the German occupation, made into a concentration camp where Jews were assembled before being despatched under appalling conditions to their deaths in Auschwitz and Sobibor in Poland and to Bergen-Belsen in Germany.

Holland was unable to remain neutral in the Second World War. On 10 May 1940 the German Blitzkrieg was launched against Holland. The Dutch forces were hopelessly outnumbered and ill-equipped to resist the overwhelming Nazi assault and Holland capitulated on 15 May 1940, one day after the devastating bombing of Rotterdam. But during those five days, Jan Albach, a reserve captain in the Dutch army, was killed on Whit Monday, 13 May 1940 during the defence of Dordrecht. His shocked family blamed him to some extent and felt that Jan had carelessly taken unnecessary risks. It was only in 2006 that Ben received an official report on his brother's death and awards for his heroism in the defence of his country.

Immediately upon German occupation, Jews began to be dismissed from all official posts and this was extended into jobs in prominent private and commercial companies as well. During the first year of the German occupation there was only a modest level of intervention in the actual running of the country but, after 1941, the occupying regime became more oppressive and brutal. Holland was, however, the only country in Europe where there were large scale demonstrations and strikes against the Nazi treatment of the Jewish population. But it did little good and it is a sad fact that Holland lost a greater proportion of its Jewish population during the Holocaust than any other European country. For those Jews who remained, life was unbelievably hard and precarious. Arnold's mother Judith died suddenly of a heart attack in 1941, undoubtedly brought on by the stress of the occupation and the rising persecution of the Jews. The three remaining members of the Noach family, father Meijer, Julia and Arnold were left in the most tenuous of situations. They could not work, their official documents, *persoonsbewijs* (identity papers) identified them as Jews by the inclusion of a 'J' (*Jood*) and they could not obtain food stamps. All those other pieces of paper which legitimized their position also identified them as Jews. They became increasingly reliant on friends who, by helping them, put their own lives at risk as well.

The anti-Jewish measures created serious tensions amongst former friends and there were fierce rows between Ben and particularly Julia, where Ben, following a row between them, wrote in his diary on 2 March 1941, 'I feel sorry for the inferiority complex from which their pride arises, but that does not alter the fact that their behaviour (toward me) was impolite.' On August 30 the quarrel was settled - with Arnold and Julia pouring out their hearts to Ben; but there was a real panic, for the persecution of the Jews was becoming increasingly serious and savage.

We have a copy of a necessarily obsequious letter which

Arnold wrote on 28 March 1941 to the Secretaris Generaal of the Department for Education, Science and Cultural Protection asking, in view of the latest regulation (which forbad Jews from attending all places of education), to be permitted to continue his doctoral studies. He received a reply on 01 April which merely told him to fill in and return the accompanying forms (in duplicate). There is no further correspondence preserved but we can guess the eventual outcome.

Ben Albach was very active in the Liberal Christian Youth Federation (VCJC) for whom he wrote, staged and acted in religious dramas, *lekespelen*, akin to a modern version of the English medieval 'Mystery Plays' but using Biblical stories to point up modern themes and often hiding within them political messages. Arnold, too was involved in these plays, even taking parts in the performances. Ben himself was also a contributor to plays which were known as Resistance Religious Dramas. Ben even directed a production of Nijhof's translation of Shakespeare's 'The Tempest' which was produced in 1940.

From this involvement in the VCJC, it became the aim to enable Arnold to be baptized as a Christian, a ruse that had become well known among many Jews who sought to obtain protection by this means. Firstly they planned for Arnold to become a member of the Liberal Christian Youth Federation as a means of protecting him from deportation. But this was forestalled, firstly by Jews being banned from being members of the VCJC and finally, the VCJC itself being dissolved.

From as early as 18 April 1941, we find from the contemporary press that a lecture which Arnold was to give to the 'Spain and Spanish-America Society' on the politics of art in the reign of King Philip the Second, was '*plotseling verhinderd*' (suddenly cancelled) but no reason is given for this in any of the press reports. We can only guess that the organizers had been ordered to cancel because their speaker was Jewish. Nevertheless, Arnold made brave attempts to continue some degree of academic and cultural normality and activities, giving art history lectures to the members of the VCJC and even taking a party on one of his famous walking lecture tours of the Oude Kerk on 14 April 1942.

On 29 April 1942, the situation of the Dutch Jews was rendered even more oppressive by the order that all Jews had to wear the yellow Star of David visible on their outer clothing. However, Ben Albach and Arnold retained their interest in the theatre and they even contrived to attend the performance of a play at the Amsterdam Stadsschouwburg, with Arnold having his arm in a sling made from a scarf to cover his Jewish Star as Jews were not allowed to attend the theatre or other places of public performance or entertainment.

Meanwhile Arnold had talked to a minister of the Roman Catholic church about the possibility of converting to Catholicism, but he moved away from this idea on the grounds that '*de kerk haalt de hemel teveel naar de aarde*' – 'the Church brings Heaven too closely down to the earth'- it is too much involved in daily life. He preferred to become a protestant and arranged for discussions toward baptism with a protestant minister. For this purpose, he moved to Veenendaal and lodged with the parents of Hebe Kohlbrugge, a resistance fighter who was a member of the Free Nederland group. There he met up again with Tetta and Arthur Wijngaard who had been guests at Arnold's celebratory dinner after the award of his doctorate in 1937 and for whom Arnold had acted as Master of ceremonies at their wedding in 1939. They were also members of the Free Nederland group. The Kohlbrugge family were strongly protestant and the grandfather of the family had been a noted protestant theologian.

Finally, on Sunday 22 February 1942, Arnold was baptized by Bernard Aris, a pastor of the more liberally inclined *Hervormde Kerk* (Reformed Church). Ben and Tetta Wijgaard were also present and Ben wrote in his diary for that date that it was 'actually a pathetic display.' Arnold hoped that he would thus acquire a baptismal stamp in his documents which would delay or even avoid deportation. But this proved useless since the occupying Nazi powers decreed that only baptismal stamps pre-dating 1942 would be accepted as evidence of religious 'conversion.' Julia was not willing to undertake this 'baptism.' On 23 February 1942, Ben wrote in his diary, 'Julia is not a Christian. She could not see the opposition of the world as God wanted her to, nor did she try to draw lessons from it.' What had intrigued Ben however, was that, a year earlier, Julia had remarked that the mockery of the Jewish Christ on the cross was so relevant and apposite to the present situation.

Both Arnold and Julia had received orders more than once to report to the camp at Westerbork, with everything that this implied, though the whole truth of the 'final solution' and the full horrors of Sobibor and Auschwitz had not yet become known in Holland by that time. Nevertheless it finally became apparent that going into hiding (onderduiken) was inevitable. Arnold and Julia and their father Meijer went into hiding and remained fugitives in their own country for the remaining three years of the war.

But not before Ben and Arnold decided to attend a festive performance given at the Stadsschouwburg. They walked through the Vossiusstraat and across the park when Arnold was suddenly overcome by a panic attack. The situation was highly dangerous with Arnold displaying his Star of David. He was already in hiding with friends in Eeghenstraat and should really not have taken the risk of going out of doors at all. Ben took him to his parents' home on Alexander Boersstraat, which greatly alarmed his mother, Cisca: "Now everyone knows where he is" she cried. Arnold had to hide in a deep chest under the window in Ben's attic room, which he shared with a clandestine radio.

On 30 September 1942 the police raided Alexander Boersstraat to search for Jews, but fortunately, no one was at home. Ben suspected that the Noachs' German maid had informed the police that Arnold was often at the Albachs. It should also be remembered that a bounty payment was offered to the police and to the public for those informing on or arresting Jews. The family of Anne Frank were informed upon and captured in the last year of the occupation and, while Ann Frank died in Bergen-Belsen, her father survived, but the informer was never identified.

Arnold had to hide his tracks and arranged with Ben to give away all his books to the mother of a friend, Otto Vos. Since she regarded them as possibly suspect and incriminating, she disposed of them over the following years. The whole library of his early years of study was lost. But we read from a letter of 22 June 1947 which he wrote to Ilse from Amsterdam that 'I have to go to the Hague for the money for my library' so he may finally have been compensated for the loss of these valuable books.

Ben busied himself trying to identify suitable places where Arnold could go into hiding (*onderduiksplaats*) and where those 'good' Dutch people involved could be relied upon for security and courage, since they were putting themselves at great risk as well by doing this. Already in hiding with friends in Eeghenstraat and then, in emergency, hiding in the Albach's own house at Alexander Boersstraat, Arnold was moved to Amersfoort to the house of the family of Frank Lulof, with whom he had been a student. Ben visited him while he was at Amersfoort and they even gave a performance of a play written by Ben and Arnold, 'Jacoba van Beieren' in which Arnold played a 'drag' part in a skirt! It was while Arnold was at the Lulof's house that he met several more resistance fighters and, it may have been from here that he himself became more closely involved in the Dutch resistance movement. As to the nature of that involvement, we know very little. The description which has come down to us today from Arnold himself and from other sources is nothing more than that he, 'did something with radio communications with Britain' and that is how it was described with little additional information at the time of his death and the writing of his various obituaries.

From this time, Arnold moved from address to address, never remaining for long in any one place, without official status and without possessions. Of this period, Arnold himself spoke very little in later life and then only to relate 'amusing' details. He told of having to hide in a very grand house where there were double doors interconnecting interior rooms and being in hiding in the space above the door lintel. Apart from the danger of his situation, there were also, not surprisingly, long periods of boredom and Arnold told how, in company with fellow fugitives, the talk would turn to food – not simply the lack of it, but detailed discussion of recipes, menus and dining which even became quite heated, with arguments as to which was the 'right' wine to serve with a particular dish, or the exact recipe for the dish. From time to time, when dining with us many years later at The Dragon House, Arnold would suddenly say, 'Ah, yes. This takes me back – and with the right wine too,' and then go on to describe the interminable discussion that the thought of this dish had provoked amongst his fellow fugitives when they themselves were near to starvation.

He made his way to Pijnacker, to the house of another member of the resistance, with Anne-Marie Bakels the Swiss wife of Floris Bakels. Floris had already been captured and was to survive several different concentration camps and spend three and a half years in captivity. First in a German prison at Scheveningen, in a prisoner transit camp at Amersfoort, a further prison at Utrecht and then in France at the notorious Natzwieler concentration camp in the Vosges. From there he was moved to further detention 'camps' and thence to Dachau in south Germany from where he was finally liberated by the advancing Americans on 29 April 1945.

That Arnold fell in love with Anne-Marie Bakels there is no

doubt. In the febrile atmosphere of war, clandestine survival and the very uncertainty of every day, it is hardly surprising. But Floris had survived and it is very much to the credit of Arnold that, on hearing that Floris had finally made it back to Holland in May 1945, and was immediately put into hospital in Maastricht by the Red Cross, and that Anne-Marie had joined him there, Arnold undertook what was, in the immediate aftermath of hostilities, an arduous and gruelling journey, the main purpose of which was to see them again. Such was Arnold's own physical condition on arrival in Maastricht that the Red Cross put him onto the same recuperation diet and regime as well, even though he had come to the hospital as a visitor. (See Arnold's undated letter written in the summer of 1945 to Julia in Amsterdam – copy in English translation).

There had been other girls in Arnold's life as well. In the calmer and more stable times of the 1930s, The Noach family had friends, the van Stempels. Father was a wholesale tobacco merchant and her mother Emma Bottenheim came from a wealthy Jewish family. They had a daughter, Henny (Henrietta) van Stempel to whom Arnold had certainly been attracted earlier on. Henny was born in Amsterdam in 1914 and was of a proud and defiant nature, which characteristics contributed to her survival throughout the war. She trained at the Barleus Gymnasium and went on to study and teach ancient languages, Latin and Greek. She was amongst the last to graduate from the University of Amsterdam in 1941 before Jews were forbidden to attend universities and schools. The Jewish communities however, took action to try to continue and to preserve education and had set up a parallel Jewish Lyceum where Henny went on to teach. She was of good family and the Noachs approved of her as a good possible match for Arnold, one of these days. Moreover, Henny's aunt was married to a leading gentile professor, Johannes Tielrooy. However, so open was professor Tielrooy's opposition to the occupation that in 1942 he was dismissed from the university and was taken and imprisoned at German prison at Amersfoort.

Henny openly taught her pupils that the Jewish Star of David should be worn with pride and communicated her pride in her faith to her students. However, by 1942 things had changed. Henny no longer had the 'academic' stamp in her papers, but she remained for the moment, exempt from the dreaded summons to Westerbork as she was identified as being in the employ of the Jewish Council and therefore had some degree of ephemeral protection.

On 6 July 1942, while she was still a student, she was arrested in a street raid as she was on her way home with her school books. She came face-to-face with the notorious SS-*Hauptsturmführer*, Aus der Fünten who snatched her books and demanded, "What's a Jewess doing with the Ancient Greeks?" She was arrested but, after being required to spend hours walking round and standing in a prison yard was, surprisingly, released the following day. In November 1942, Henny's parents were taken from their home in Amsterdam and sent separately, her mother to Sobibor where she was murdered while her father was sent to Theresienstadt, which he survived. This type of bizarre lottery of survival came about because Henny's father had a 'baptismal' stamp in his persoonsbewijs (identity papers) while her mother's had not yet been entered. Such were the slimmest of threads by which the lives of people hung during the occupation.

In the absence of her parents, Henny's house was ransacked and valuable paintings and antiques disappeared, never to be recovered. She went to live with her uncle, Johannes Tielrooy and continued to teach at the Jewish Lyceum. She lived there for six months in company with the Tielrooy's daughter, Jettie, who had been dismissed from her teaching post as she was a teacher of French (now forbidden).

Jettie Tielrooy had found work at a local bookshop where she sold 'under the counter' Chassidic prints and work by Jewish philosophical writers for which there was still, even then, a demand. The works of Martin Buber could be obtained there, as could illegally forged *persoonbewijsen* and food stamps. It is certainly the case that, through this connection, Henny came to know the work of the protestant theologian Kornelis Miskotte and attended his services where he was courageous enough to include the statutory royal prayers for Queen Wilhelmina, who, with her government, was in exile in London.

But in spite of all the stamps provided by the Jewish Council, which until then had provided protection against deportation, Henny left Amsterdam. She went into hiding with the Laarmans, a protestant family in Leiden. There she continued her contacts with Christianity and was finally baptized into the Dutch Reformed Church in October 1944 by the Rev. Touw, the brother-in-law of the Rev. Miskotte. So, throughout all the period of the German occupation of the Netherlands, there was a continuing undercurrent of religious philosophical activity, resulting in the those baptisms, those losses and finding of faith and of people simply trying to lead their lives without the savage and barbaric interventions of the occupying Germans.

Henny van Stempel and Arnold Noach had to go their separate ways in order to survive and, quite simply, they drifted apart along the currents of war and of the occupation.

It is almost impossible to trace, after over 75 years, exactly where Arnold spent those years on the run. We know from the reminiscences of Francine Albach, Ben's daughter, some of the places where Arnold managed to stay, but as to the sequence of his movements or the time spent at each of the places about which we know, we will never now be certain. We do know that he moved about a great deal and it is surprising that, at a time when there were guards at every railway station and squads of the occupying Germans plucking out at random for questioning travellers from any passing group, that as far as we know, Arnold was never arrested. In one 'near miss,' he was at a house when a search squad arrived. There was in the house an old man in bed. He was summarily turned out, the mattress lifted and Arnold thrust underneath and the old man got back in on top of him. He said that it was a close-run thing as to whether he suffocated before the search squad gave up and left.

He came through the war at least physically unscarred. What such a life does to the mental constitution of any but the most resilient and hard-minded is entirely another matter. It is interesting to make the comparison with the wartime life of his friend Floris Bakels who, over thirty years later, committed the events of his war years to print in his book, 'Nacht und Nebel.' He survived on a combination of sheer physical toughness, enduring love for his wife and a deep religious conviction which appears never to have flinched in the face of almost unimaginable horrors. But he was exceptional and not everyone can hope to be like that.

Arnold survived. When the country was liberated, he made his way back to Amsterdam 'from the south, by boat' he said, and met up again with his father and his sister, both of whom had miraculously managed to evade the rounding-up, the deportation and murder of over 75% of the pre-war Jewish population of a country where the Jews had been an integral part of the structure, the fabric and the culture of the country for over four centuries. In later life Arnold only spoke of his wartime life in Holland in brief fragments and of his involvement with the Dutch resistance as having something to do with radio communication with Britain.

Arnold was able to 'reappear' soon after the final liberation of the country on 5 May 1945. In an un-dated letter to his sister Julia, in 1945, Arnold describes the beginning of returning to freedom and life again. The journey to Maastricht made during the summer of 1945 also appears to have had the purpose of simply finding out what had happened their friends and relatives and to the assets of the family in various places around the country. Arnold went to Maastricht to see the Bakels, but also via Nijmegen where he found the town in ruins. Appalling damage had been done when it was mistakenly bombed during the abortive 'Operation Market Garden,' the attempt to establish a bridgehead over the Rhine during the Allied advance into Germany. In this letter, Arnold describes in his usual 'amusing' way, the difficulties of travel and accommodation during his trip and at one point, he is able to write, 'Darling. I feel that I'm alive!'

Similarly, in his letter to Ilse of 17 October 1951, Arnold has no need to explain why he had gone to Paris, but he writes 'our affairs are in good order at last after 6½ years of haggling and conferring and letter writing' and of extracting family funds from the Paris branch of the Netherlands Bank.

After the war, Julia returned from Leiden to Amsterdam, apparently living in the old family house at Valeriusstraat with her father. She did not resume her former life as a concert pianist and appears, over the following years to have led a withdrawn, lonely life, alone in the big house.

In Arnold's letter to Julia of summer 1945, he mentions having been told that Julia's concert grand piano had been given into safe keeping with 'Heymans' and both Arnold and the Bakels are insistent that the piano should be returned, as it was not a gift but merely handed on for safe-keeping. Arnold and the Bakels say it should be returned to 'Rapenburg.' This is an elegant street in Leiden, tree-lined and overlooking a canal. Number 51, is a handsome tall Dutch house of probably eighteenth century construction, and it does appear to have been, at some point, where the Bakels lived but, possibly owned by Meijer Noach as one of his several properties.

The war had also affected Julia in a way that I recognize all too well. Francine Albach felt sorry for her and describes going with her sisters to dinner with Julia years later where she cooked a chicken. When they left, Julia gave them the remains of the chicken and the bones, as it had become engraved on the conscience of so many people that no food could ever be wasted if it could possibly be kept, cached and eaten later.

In 1946, Arnold was 'sent' to England by Mrs. Bé Siemens of Leiden with whom Julia had been in hiding. She sent Arnold off to England 'because the food is better there' and, in his own, light-hearted, self-deprecating words, he 'came on holiday in 1946 and never went home again.'

4

LETTER FROM ARNOLD
TO HIS SISTER JULIA

Undated, but from high summer 1945

The following letter was written by Arnold to his sister Julia in high summer of 1945 when he travelled to the far south of Holland to Maastricht in Limburg. We do not know whether the original of the letter has survived or who made this translation into English, obtained from Paul Hellmann. It gives us an interesting insight into Arnold's ability to 'get going' again and to do one of the things which he enjoyed – to travel, observe and comment. It would appear from the text that Julia knew Floris Bakels better then Arnold did. Floris Bakels had been liberated from the concentration camp at Dachau is south Germany only a short time before and had made his way back to Holland where he was picked up by the Red Cross and put into hospital to recuperate. He had spent nearly three and a half years in various concentration camps before he was freed.

The letter also tells us something of the prevailing conditions and of Arnold's state of mind.

The M G which he mentions was the temporary Militair Gezag, Netherlands Military Authority, which was tasked with enforcing curfews and issuing special permits for certain businesses or travel.

My dear sister,

Arrived at Maastricht at 3 in the afternoon, went straight to the hospital and spent from 3.30 to 6 (or longer) talking to Floris. What an interesting chap! His condition is less serious than assumed, he's become fat and has a double chin, wants to quietly (....) and wait for his complete recovery, to some time later undergo the emotions of his work, your music and other exciting things, tells everything very calmly about the camps and all the suffering, speaks of literature and art, without it ever seeming to wear him out (of course I wanted to go away after half an hour, but he absolutely wouldn't let me). Anne-Marie is ecstatic and has also grown fat, stuffs herself silly (*this is a colloquial expression in Dutch, 'eet zich een ongeluk.' Lit: 'eats herself an accident*). But she goes on about how she has saddened you (*let you down*), doesn't know how to make it up.

For the time being (or really not at all) not returning to Leiden. She begs you to have the grand piano come to R'burg (*Obviously* Rapenburg, *not known to the original translator*). Floris and she says that Heymans has no right at all, although it would be advisable to talk to him. They intend to terminate (*check out*) at Boekweit (*name of the hospital where they were*) probably by the 1st of September, having an eye on a dwelling at the Brouwersgracht and are also discussing the possibility of living together with you, but take my advice and don't mind the money and stay at the wonderful Rapenburg and come and stay as often as you like and whenever you like, in Amsterdam.

We had stage fright for the reunion; for I am the first from the north received by Floris. But it went well and we directly had a good contact. He thinks I look like Max Orobio de C. (*unknown name*) which, I believe, is meant as a compliment.

In the hospital, I pass as the cousin of Anne-Marie's (and all the nurses say there's an obvious likeness!) who is here on behalf of Floris' business, since that's the only way to make the hospital look after me. I eat at the hospital (Anne-Marie serves it to me herself, so you'll understand I'm short of nothing!) and I sleep, for the moment free, at the W. Sprenger family's. Surprisingly their son Jan, architecture-historian, turns out to be an acquaintance of mine whom I intended to visit anyway! Address: Mrs. W. Sprenger, St. Hubertuslaan, Maastricht, but I will have left when you receive this letter. They pamper me thoroughly, lovely house, beautiful room. All this is a great relief to me in many ways.

Now for the report of my journey to this place, silly and adventurous as everything I witness. In my usual tormentingly slow manner I arrived yesterday only after eight at the Museumplein (*Amsterdam*) where a military transport awaited me. (Have you already heard that the other day in Leiden, after a conversation that lasted an hour, I finally managed at the M.G. to get a permit out of the hands of Mr. Udo de Haes. Heavens, I had to open the flood-gates of my eloquence, poor Haes! It was almost animal-mistreatment – third degree under which he almost collapsed.) At 9 o'clock I suddenly discovered a car went to Nijmegen. Departure: 9.15, arrival 11.30. An incredible achievement on the part of the driver. Enormously kind chaps, who gave me many cigarettes, bread and meat, cake and other delicious things. In Nijmegen, which has become unrecognizable, alas! It was too late to notify the (Balgans/Balsans??? *Sorry, can't make out – note by original translator*), so I asked overnight to stay at the… police office, that in this hotel-less and almost houseless city usually takes care of strangers. There I got a straw mattress in a somewhat stuffy space, with no pillow or blanket in the very mixed company of seven other hobo's, who did not scruple to anything, but at least they were – *grâce au ciel* – free of vermin which, in the surrounding atmosphere there, apparently had no chance of surviving. Reception very jovial by the way. Company of policemen, very generous with cigarettes, coffee and bread, now and then illuminated by visits of the prisoners who were let out of their cells due to the warm weather. Little sleep but lots of fun. In the morning at 6, I was pulled at my, apparently thereto serving, right foot by officer on duty. Wash, shave and breakfast, at 7 seven start working. At 8.30 military vehicle to Roermond,

Nijmegen, 1945

Trouble there: the south is ruled by the Americans who have little faith in permits of the M.G. Opened flood-gates of eloquence over American officer, who bent under the force, poor chap, and took me with him to Sittard. Over there, mesmerized a patrolling agent of the US Military Police, who loyally held up a car to Maastricht for me, full of negroes who felt honoured and brought me almost all the way to the hospital, in spite of the fact that it was out of their way.

Anne-Marie now has a room in the house of Mrs. de Nerée tot Babberich, shitty posh, no less than a palace. She mingles by the way in the best of Maastricht circles, which becomes her.

Darling, I feel I'm alive. But what misery with all this destruction around, it's sad.

I stop now for I'm tumbling with sleep. Bye bye.

Nolletje (*Little Nol*)

5

ENGLAND AND BEYOND

Arnold was 'sent' to England by Mrs. Bé (Beatrice) Siemens of Leiden with whom Julia (and possible also her father) had been in hiding. She packed Arnold off to England 'because the food is better there.' This is ironic because, as we Britons now remember it, the availability of food and the level of British rations was actually reduced in the immediate aftermath of the war. However, this was shortly after the Hunger Winter in Holland and the fact of there being even adequate, closely controlled food supplies on which to survive must have appealed to any Dutch person coming to England at that time.

Arnold appears to have been able very easily to gain entry to the country and to settle here. There is a suggestion here that his arrival in the country was facilitated as a reward for his work for the British in clandestine radio communications from occupied Holland and it is significant that he was almost immediately involved with the BBC and gave talks on the new

Third Programme and on the BBC World Service Dutch section. We know very little of exactly what his radio activities had been. He himself had referred *en passant* that he 'did a bit with radio communication with Britain' but he said no more than that. We have also had that confirmed from other sources but, understandably, like all clandestine and underground work, there are no records and no further explanations.

It is not surprising that Arnold decided to stay in England and ultimately to make this country his home for the rest of his life. He appears to have been put in touch with Ilse Hellmann very soon after his arrival in the country. This may have been on the basis of some expatriate mutual support network among survivors from the occupation of Holland and also the connection via Bé Siemens to the Hellmann family who were close friends from

The Family Hellmann, 1930. Ilse Hellmann second from the right (front row)

pre-war years. As early as January 1947 we find Arnold, having returned to Holland to sort out family affairs, writing to Ilse that 'I long to be back in London (to you?) where I feel I belong more than here. Amsterdam is as lovely as ever, but as I told you some time ago, I can't visualize myself as a permanent resident again.'

It is more likely (and there is evidence to support this) that Arnold first came to Ilse in her professional capacity through her work with remedial psychiatric help for displaced persons, although her main area of operation was with children who had been evacuated and displaced within this country and were disturbed as a result. Arnold and Ilse met very soon after he arrived and settled in London. He had, as he told the story, a 'bed-sit' in a divided up house. In one of the other rooms he found a shop-window female mannequin. He dragged this back to his room and, when Ilse called, he deliberately left it partly hidden under his bed with a pair of feet in high-heeled shoes sticking out. He did not relate how Ilse reacted but this was typical of the sort of 'high-jinks' practical joke which amused him and typified the sheer joy of being free for many of the survivors of the worst excesses of the war. A taste for silly pranks was so often a release for many who found that you could actually 'have fun' again. As Arnold had written to his sister in 1945, 'I feel that I'm alive!'

Arnold had connections. His broadcasts on the BBC Third Programme were brought to the notice of Kenneth Clarke, the Surveyor of the King's Pictures. Through him he was offered the job of participating in the cataloguing of the old master drawings in the Royal Collections at Windsor and continued in this work under Clarke's successor, Anthony Blunt, with whom Arnold did not get on. His main contribution was to identify those drawings of Italian architectural scenes where he was able, through his enormous knowledge of Italy and its art, to identify both artists and scenes which he recognized from his travels and places of study.

In 1948 we find Arnold travelling in Italy and writing to Ilse from the British School in Rome, on very poor quality paper (all he could get hold of) and in tiny, crabbed writing to cram as much as possible onto the small pieces. In June of 1948, he tells Ilse (whom he now addresses as 'Darling') that 'returning to Rome now means finding the same place but a slightly different person.' That 'slightly different person' is very much an understatement and it was left to Ilse in her professional capacity to assess just how much Arnold had recovered and had changed during the war and in his memory of Rome and Italy from his travels in the 1920s and 1930s. He continues, 'It is so marvellous to be there, to see everything and touch everything that one cannot find words for it.'

He made some of his re-acquainting visits in company with the art historian Hugo Buchthal whom he met in Rome. But Arnold reported that Buchthal 'feels rather unhappy in [the] English surroundings [of the Warburg Institute]. The Warburg Institute, founded by Aby Warburg, had been based in Hamburg but in 1934, the then guardians had managed to ship the whole contents of its library and collections to England, where it was re-established before becoming in 1944, a free-standing School within London University. Hugo Buchthal was, with E H Gombrich and Nicholas Pevsner, one of a number of refugee art historians who had made England their home. 'Buchthal told me that he would like me to become a fellow, 'so I need not spend my time and thought on journalism." However, Arnold continues, 'it would be nice, especially if it came true, but I have seen too many mice born from mountains already.' He was later to write, 'Buchthal has left, moved to a flat a friend lent him. He is rather a peculiar fellow, not bad, but very German. He does everything to impress his good character on people. Well I wonder. But to talk to he is very nice, informative, ready to laugh. I will tell you more about everything when we meet.' Arnold was pleased to be able to report to Ilse that, 'my work proceeds not too badly. At the Vatican *mss.* dept. they have a less than I had expected but Monday I start at the state archives where they promised me a lot.'

Obviously Arnold was returning to his habits of scholarship and research and was rejoicing in their therapeutic effects. Many of the letters which he wrote to Ilse at this time appear to be, in an indirect way, reporting on his 'recovery' to a psychotherapist with whom he was also very much in love. On 21 June 1948 he wrote to Ilse, 'Again the paper is bad but my mood is good. After 2½ weeks I am settled down now and I don't believe I lose an hour a day on useless things. Breakfast at 8 or 8.30., then to some archive or library along the lovely sloping avenues of the Villa Borghese down to the piazza del Popolo, you know the one that opens onto three streets like this [*and a tiny illustrative doodled sketch in the margin*] and so to work. Usually I visit a handful of churches on my way (the little buggers who keep them are only open in the morning and at night). Lunch at 1; then out again, forced walk and then to the Instituto del Storia dell'Arte for which I have a ticket – that's open until 8. Then dinner, like all meals I take it at the School, then an hour's work, a long walk, a glass of wine, again some work, and so to bed, usually at 2 in the morning. A pleasantly busy life.'

Inevitably there were those 'happenings' which were so very typically Arnold. In the Lawrence family we actually coined an adjective 'Arnoldian' to describe them. 'For the rest,' he wrote, 'there are the usual crazy things as they only happen to me. This morning, for example, I was working at documents in the sacristy of the church La Maddelena (a delightful little Baroque church near the Pantheon, begun by Carlo Fontana but only partly built after his designs.) Suddenly the door opened and a nervous girl burst into the room and asked whether she could be admitted to confession (it was an almost completely dark room and all she saw of me was my bald head!) When I told her that I could not tell her so, she got into a rage, from which I gathered that confession was very much needed, but admission to it was doubtful. So I called one of the brothers of the Order (St. Camillus) to which the church belongs.'

He writes to Ilse again from Amsterdam on 26 June 1948 to tell her that he has been turned down for a post in 'Extra-Mural Studies' [*he does not say at what institution*] but is able to comment that 'it is a pity I haven't got anything fixed next year. I really don't know where my optimism comes from. Am I going really [to] need this time? If so it is a pleasant process for never since I was 25 have I felt so thoroughly alive.....Altogether I believe I have been doing quite a lot, especially in the way of relaxation. But even working time has yielded some results.'

In a brief note on 7 July from Rome, 'a little letter on filthy paper' Arnold tells Ilse 'I shall stay here until the 15th, the date the whole Vatican show closes down and no more work can be done. I think I shall get ready and I believe I have used my time [well] to a certain extent.' But he also asks Ilse in the same letter to 'tell me more about your atrocious journey on the continent.' This may well have been Ilse's start on the grim forensic historical journey taken up by Paul Hellmann in his search for the fate of so many members of the Hellmann family.

On 10 July Arnold sends Ilse a telegram 'Rome until Friday Florence Umbria Venice week each if money.' So he was, as in his former, pre-war life, roaming Italy and its endless store of art and art history, partly as a therapy and reporting on it and his mood and reactions back to Ilse, one can conjecture, as part of his recovery.

On 29 July Arnold writes to Ilse from a small *pensione* in Florence by now addressing her as 'My own darling' and beginning with 'It seems ages since I wrote to you last.' His letter is a joyous travelogue from what is now a distant time. 'Assisi was lovely, just a dream of medieval life; I shall never forget it. The church of San Francesco with frescos by Giotto, the hilly country all around, all the monasteries and sloping streets, everything blue and grey.'

And in Urbino on a Sunday, he writes that 'everything was closed' so he went down to the sea and swam. 'It was marvellous, the blue Adriatic, a cool wind and almost warm water. Nobody on the beach and complete freedom.' It is worthy of note, but not surprising how often that word 'freedom' crops up in his writing at this time. In that same letter he writes, 'I really believe I shall get the Windsor Catalogue ready be the end of this year; I found much material that it finally covers the whole.'

In a final letter in this series, Arnold writes from the old family home in Valeriusstraat in Amsterdam, 'I now feel completely rested and full of beans.' He also writes hopefully, 'Gombrich in Amsterdam and talks future (Nol-future). He also tells Ilse, 'I bought lots of books, 2000 Guilders worth. All things I needed and once possessed......For the rest [*of his visit and meetings in Holland*] I enjoyed being 'of it' and not 'in it." He concludes to Ilse, written to her flat in Belsize Park, 'If you hear someone panting up the stairs and dropping cases all over the place, it's me.'

From his continuing work at Windsor, he wrote short articles for the *Burlington Magazine* in 1949 on the wall paintings in San Clemente and, in 1956 on the tomb of Pope Paul III, while in the pre-war period, he had contributed articles on one of Rembrandt's last, unfinished paintings, 'Julius Civilis' to academic journals, *De Gids* in 1937 and *Oude Amsterdam* in 1939.

He did not finish at Windsor by the end of the year 1948 as he once hoped and intended and the cataloguing work continued slowly and intermittently into the 1950s and resulted in a set of typed index cards, often annotated in Arnold's own hand, which, to this day remain in the archives at Windsor. Various other catalogues of sections of the drawing collections have since been published, with Arnold's contribution acknowledged where it was appropriate, but, as the present Head of Prints and Drawings at the Royal collections wrote to me, 'a comprehensive and specific catalogue of *The Italian Architectural Drawings in the Collection of Her Majesty The Queen at Windsor Castle* never saw the light of day.

Unfortunately, as with so many of Arnold's projects and scholastic participations in the post-war years, he proved dilatory and, quite simply, did not get on with the job. Toward the end of his time at Windsor, a letter about the situation, by Sir Owen Morshead (Royal Librarian up to 1958) to Anthony Blunt in 1955 states, 'Our talk was conducted along a friendly plane, and I urged him to help me not to have recourse afresh to forms of pressure distasteful to us both.'

Nevertheless, shortly after this, Arnold left (or was discretely dismissed) from the job, when he became a lecturer in art history at Leeds University in 1956. Arnold joined the department of fine art at Leeds when it was in a state of flux, or more precisely, in a state of near withering away altogether. The department was a new venture for the university and had been set up only a few years before in 1949 at the instigation of the art critic and writer, Herbert Read, author of 'Education through Art,' and Bonamy Dobrée, professor of English at Leeds.

At its outset, the department consisted of just two people. The first of these was the head of the department, Maurice de Sausmarez, a Channel Islander originally from Guernsey, an extremely good artist but more than a little distrait in his daily life.

The other was a lecturer in art history, a sullen Austro-Hungarian Marxist, Arnold Hauser, who lectured in a dull, flat, guttural accent and was one of the most boring lecturers it has ever been my misfortune to encounter. He was stolid and bald and would drone on as he showed a series of slides in a darkened, warm lecture theatre which was dreadfully conducive to slumber during afternoon lectures. On one occasion, he slammed the lid of the lectern and in rising volume in his thick accent, screeched, 'I am not minding vhen you are schleeping in my lectures, but vhen you are schnoring I can't schtand it!'

Hauser was also of a lecherous disposition and girl students made a point of keeping a safe distance away from his lubricious approaches, even to the extent of taking a chaperone with them when invited to his study to 'discuss their latest essay.' One girl in my year took along a large, muscular, theology student friend who was a member of the university first XV rugby team and who would sit, stony-faced for each hour without saying a word as he quietly read. Even the egregious Hauser must have understood. Hauser left at the end of the university year in 1956 and was replaced by Arnold Noach. As he said at his interview when asked to assess his own suitability for the position, 'I'm another bald foreigner called Arnold.'

Under Maurice de Sausmarez, the department was never going to function properly and so a secretary was appointed to 'hold things together' while the university senate decided where the department of fine art was to go. Miss Margaret Field came in 1956 and she and Arnold got on well together. Meanwhile Maurice became more and more unstable and out of this world in a harmless, charming and fay sort of way. Even in 1954-55, when I was a student of the department for just one subsidiary year, it was not unusual for Maurice to fail to turn up at all for his lectures. We would have a whip-round for the tram fare for someone to go to his house in Headingley to find out where he was. On more than one occasion, he came to the door in an artist's smock with a palette and brushes in his hand and said, in astonishment, "Good Heavens! Is it Thursday?"

Toward the end of Maurice's time at Leeds, Arnold became

so concerned about his mental state that he worried about Margaret, saying, "Are you sure it's safe being left alone with him?" Of course it was; Maurice was gravely mentally ill but remained totally 'safe' and quite gently charming throughout all of his time in Leeds.

Maurice left to go into full-time psychiatric treatment. He achieved a complete recovery and went on to a post as principal of the Byam Shaw School of Art in Kensington,. Among his students was a young man who had pretensions to becoming an 'artist' but Maurice could see that he did not have the essential talent for that and would never make it in the world of art. He called him in one day and told him to forget the 'artist' side and concentrate instead on industrial design for which he had a real, genuine flair. James Dyson went on to design vacuum cleaners.

When Maurice left Leeds, the university had to decide on the future of the department. What they wanted was a fine art department which would grow, be properly run and administered and become a serious, major part of the arts function of the University and which would offer three-year degree and post-graduate courses instead of only the subsidiary and single-year courses that it had up to that time. Arnold, of course, wanted the head job and worked hard and lobbied to try and get it. In truth, he would not have been suitable for the job that the university wanted done. He was a scholar and a remarkably knowledgeable connoisseur of art and architecture and an inspired lecturer, but he was not an administrator, an organizer or a leader, which was what the university needed.

At this time, Arnold even considered buying a house in Leeds and he and Ilse had looked at a rather charming Regency villa on Potternewton Lane in Chapel Allerton, but did not buy. We, the Lawrences, also looked at that same house some years later when we were house hunting but settled for something more modest, but considerably more convenient in Headingley.

The university chose rightly, a very different sort of candidate for the post of professor of fine art, Quentin Bell, who was appointed in 1957. He was warned beforehand that the professorship would have the problem of a frustrated top man to deal with and this continued to be a difficulty and *leitmotif* of the department throughout the next decade.

Arnold was understandably hurt and frustrated by the choice. And it was even worse on a personal level. Quentin Bell was a member of the 'Bloomsbury Group,' that collection of egotistical philanderers who, as Dorothy Parker succinctly put it, 'lived in squares, painted in circles and loved in triangles.' He had no formal qualifications of any sort. He had been to school at the Leighton Park Quaker school for a few years as a boy and nothing formal beyond that except to be immersed in the self-regarding narcissism of Bloomsbury. For a continental European, it must have been perverse and bizarre in the extreme to have a man with no recognized, formal qualifications of any sort promoted over you.

Moreover, Quentin Bell had suffered tuberculosis as a young man and had been declared unfit for military service and so contrived so sit out the war in the depths of the countryside. Arnold, on the other hand, having no choice in the matter, had led a life of hardship and danger and the risk of imminent death, for several years together. Meanwhile Quentin had been living on a farm in rural Sussex while the war for our liberty and the very survival of the country was being waged a few thousand feet above his head as young men in their Spitfires and Hurricanes fought the Battle of Britain. The Dutch were, and still are, very conscious of the sacrifice which Britain made throughout the war and Arnold must have felt that Quentin Bell had 'short-changed' his country by failing to contribute at all to that effort. It was not a good start to an academic relationship. Arnold was able to cope and wrote to Ilse in October 1961, 'We are jogging along fine in the department and the Stimmung (*Ger.* atmosphere) couldn't be better.

He was even invited by Quentin and Olivia Bell to dinner at their house at Shadwell when one of the other guests was the Lord Mayor or York. That could have been a useful point from which Arnold could have extended his architectural and art historical work to York Minster but there is no record that he did so. Ilse and Maggie came to Leeds in the same October and they invited the Bells to lunch at a dining room in the university staff house, so there was a reasonable social interchange.

Arnold found much to enjoy during his time in Leeds. He lectured and taught only for a part of each week in term time. When in Leeds, he had rooms in Devonshire Hall which afforded him some of that feeling of stylish Oxford and Cambridge collegiate life which he and his friends had sought after during their careers at the University of Amsterdam in the 1930s. 'Devon' with its stone quadrangles and mullioned windows and its gowned formality must have seemed almost out of another world for someone whose quite recent life had been so precarious.

The hall consisted of a series of lawned quadrangles and had incorporated two pre-existing large houses when it was built in the late 1920s. Arnold was at first given lodgings in the suite of guest rooms in one of these, the Warden's house, which interconnected with the main hall via an enclosed cloister which also led to the kitchens and backstairs working areas. He related how, returning late to hall after an evening out, he found that the door through which he normally entered that part of the hall had been locked. He thought that, if he could gain access to the kitchen area, he could certainly get through into the house. He found a conveniently open window and, hoisting himself up onto the sill, stepped down into the darkness of the kitchen – ankle deep into a sink full of water and newly peeled potatoes.

He extricated himself and retired, leaving a mysterious trail of wet footprints from kitchen to guest rooms.

Devonshire Hall, Leeds University

I remember that we had a number of dining hall maids at Devon who came from southern Italy and had little grasp of English. On one occasion Arnold, finding that the breakfast toast had gone soft, explained this in Italian to one of the maids and asked for some fresh. The words that we caught were, 'il toast è morbido.' 'Morbid toast' became and remained a part of our family vocabulary thereafter.

In Devon, Arnold tended to seek out the company of the younger members, students rather than the various staff members and other academics who lived there. One is reminded of Mr. Pickwick, a jolly fellow with his accompanying younger companions around him to whom he is the older advisor, facilitator and wise friend. He was often to be found in the evening amongst a group of students when someone had volunteered, 'Coffee in my room after dinner.' I learnt a great deal of extra art history from him in these informal discussions and casual excursions into the byways of European art.

Quentin Bell got on with the task of developing the department of fine art and recruited a very new and rather shy graduate of the Courtauld Institute, Eric Cameron and a painter, John Jones from the local adult education college, Swarthmore. Much later both of these were told by outsiders that they had acted as a vital buffer and peace-keepers between Quentin and Arnold. And Margaret Field developed a reputation for being extremely diplomatic to the extent that she later learnt that she was referred to, behind her back, as 'Sir Humphrey' after the suave, politically-savvy civil servant, Sir Humphrey Appleby, in the contemporary television political sit-com, 'Yes, Minister.'

On one occasion, Quentin Bell, who wanted to complete some piece of written work, gave Margaret strict instructions that he was not, under any circumstances to be disturbed. "You sit here and protect me. Be a dragon," he said. The name stuck and expanded into other fields. Margaret became and was known for the rest of her life as 'The Dragon' to friends and family and even in the name of every house where we have lived – 'The Dragon House.' I have even found among Margaret's effects, a personal letter to our son Julian and myself which is simply signed, 'Dragon.' But she would always explain, 'It's not a very fierce Dragon.'

Margaret recounted that one of the severe drawbacks of

working with Quentin was that, as a result of the treatment then used for tuberculosis, Quentin had spent years being given the then widely used out-of-doors treatment of living in brutally cold conditions. As a result, he was apparently totally immune to cold. Margaret would go to work in a heavy fur coat and if asked in to help correcting proofs or taking dictation, she would first get fully dressed up in fur coat, fur hat and warm boots before going in to Quentin's room where he would be working in mid-winter in his shirt-sleeves with the heating off and the windows wide open in his sixth-floor, pent-house office.

It was Arnold Noach who, inadvertently, first introduced me to Margaret. During one of those leisurely after-dinner discussions at Devonshire Hall, some information was mentioned and I said, "I'll look that up for you and drop it into your office." "I may not be there tomorrow," replied Arnold. "But if I'm not, see my secretary. You'll like her," he said. That was in my last year at Leeds, 1957-58 and, for the next year, I would travel whenever I could from the Midlands where I was then working, to Leeds for weekends together with Margaret. I took a job in Bradford in 1959 and we were married in 1961. Our son, Julian was born in 1963 and Arnold was his godfather, together with Jill Rennie, a long-standing family friend and my younger brother Peter who, by then was

Julian's Christening
Arnold, Jill Rennie, Peter Lawrence

a student of biochemistry at Leeds and also living in Devonshire Hall. Peter went on to a distinguished academic research career which took him all over the world and toward the end of his academic career to a senior research post at the University of Hohenheim Stuttgart in Germany.

Arnold did, however, have one significant problem as a lecturer. When one considers that, during the occupation of the Netherlands, he had been active in radio communication with Britain, it is strange that Arnold and the technology of communication never seemed to be compatible. Every time he tried to use it, it turned round and bit him. As slide projectors became widely used in lecture theatres, they came initially with a long wire connection to a hand-set which the lecturer could operate to change the slides. One of his students relates how Arnold would trail this to the front of the lecture theatre and, while talking would turn from screen to lectern and back again, always in the same rotational direction. After he had done this a few times he had to be 'un-wound' again from the encircling wire with the help of his students. It was not conducive to concentration nor to the gravitas what he was saying. Famously, on another occasion, he was equipped with a new system, a hand microphone and radio operated slide changer. However much he poked at tinkered with it, no sound could be produced over the speaker system. At last Margaret had to be sent for to sort matters out and she arrived at the lecture theatre just at the same time as another lecturer from an adjacent theatre arrived to say that, every time Arnold spoke, his voice came booming out over the speaker system in *his* theatre. Margaret, Cambridge philosopher and pupil of Ludwig Wittgenstein, applied logic to the situation. She swapped over the hand-sets between the two lecture theatres and then Arnold could be heard in his theatre and his neighbour could continue his lecture uninterrupted.

In 1963, Arnold was invited to the United States to give

a series of courses, initially for a term at Pennsylvania State University. While there, he wrote prolifically to Ilse and his now teenage daughter Margaret in London. He was writing one or two letters a week, describing the place, the set-up, his work and courses and the oddities of life in a new and, at times, very different environment. It is evident that he was enjoying it and was very much taken with the setting and his reception by both the students and other members of staff. By the time he had been at Penn State for a couple of months, the department was seriously discussing the possibility of having a separate professorship of art history and this continued as a discussion, a counting of the funds and a general serious consideration for the whole of his first sojourn in Pennsylvania. They wanted to keep Arnold in America. Indeed, as early as February 1964, he was asked whether, if funds could be found within their budgets, he would want to stay there as professor of art history. But with the Noach's new house at Drayton Gardens, the situation with regard to Ilse's own extremely important career in psychotherapy, their daughter Margaret's education and a real yearning on Arnold's part to be in England, the matter continued as a discussion throughout that first stay. However, it appears to have been decided by the inability of the university to afford the extra salary of a further professor.

Apart from his obvious encyclopædic knowledge of European art and architecture, Arnold must have personified, for the Americans, the perfect European art connoisseur – the formality of dress, the English accent spiced with a slight, indefinable 'foreign' finesse, the boundless knowledge and enthusiasm for works and places which still seemed for so many Americans, a sort of strange, exotic Valhalla far beyond their shores. He was much liked and each visit was a new invitation for the students and post-graduates to avail themselves of the extraordinary cornucopia of his knowledge.

Arnold's first period at Penn State had coincided with the move from their house at Wellington Square to Drayton Gardens and his letters are full of discussions, instructions, caveats and details regarding the fitting out, decoration and furnishing of the new house and the moving of all his library and academic possessions. Throughout this period his letters are full of endless details of his life in America, his work and his contacts with a wide range of friends and contacts who were a part of the post-war refugee diaspora to the United States.

He led an extremely busy life of intensive work and local travel between Pennsylvania, New York and Philadelphia. He was also invited to give public lectures at Princeton in New Jersey and at the University of Milwaukee. He describes his lecture at Princeton given on the day after St. Patrick's day, 'which as you know is rather jolly in America. Lots of green paint, etc. On the platform of that vast hall where I spoke stood, next to me, a huge cast of the Farnese Hercules. The students had put green paint on its privy parts and it looked quite unusual, rather catholic and liturgical.'

He also described the unusual custom at Princeton, dating back to the eighteenth century, which allowed students to have pet dogs in college. As he lectured, a dog sauntered casually into the hall, sat down at the front, crossed its paws, and remained there throughout the lecture, occasionally scratching itself but otherwise paying attention. When the lecture was over, the dog located its owner and the two left together.

At Leeds and also at Penn State, Arnold's most rewarding activity was to take a party of students on a day out or on a short tour to look at and discuss architecture in the field, usually to some special building or location, or sometimes to take in a whole town or even just a row of interesting houses. His enormous range of knowledge, his eye for detail and his enthusiasm for his subject made these excursions some of the best manifestations of his connoisseurship and his ability to explain and enthuse his audience.

I remember going for a walk with him one summer's evening after dinner, locally around the pleasant, leafy Victorian suburban streets in Leeds where Devonshire Hall was located. I received a memorable lecture on nineteenth century domestic architecture, the details of which I can recall to this day. But such was his enthusiasm that he was known to trample, quite without any intention of being impolite, over the social niceties or even the privacy of anyone whose house or premises were of interest to him. On that memorable evening walk around Headingley, he boldly walked up the garden path of a private house where the owners were sitting out on the lawn in the evening sunshine. 'Please don't mind us,' said Arnold, 'I'm just explaining an architectural point to my friend here.' By the time he had finished, he had gained two more members of an enthralled audience who thanked him profusely, saying, 'Well, I know more about our house now than I ever thought I would be able to learn.'

With a party in Italy of which my by then fiancée Margaret was a member, Arnold led his group into an 'interesting' medieval hospital where he stood in the middle of an occupied ward, expatiating on its history and architecture to the great consternation of the staff. And we remembered throughout our lives his excursion to that northern Baroque palace, Castle Howard. For some strange reason, Arnold could not understand that, by a quirk of our language, it was Castle Howard – and not Howard Castle. 'Howard Castle' it became every time he mentioned it by name and that is what stuck in our minds ever after. In preparation for this biography, I called a friend, now in her nineties, who was of that party. 'Oh,' she said, 'Howard Castle. I remember it well.'

Margaret had met Arnold's sister Julia on a number of occasions and, in 1961, the year that we were to marry, she invited Margaret to come and stay with her in Amsterdam and to explore the city and, more importantly, spend time in the Rijksmuseum. Margaret had stretched her vacation allowance to its limits and beyond for our wedding and honeymoon to be spent among the chateaux and vineyards of the Loire valley and did not feel able to ask for more time off. Later,

JuliaNoach, Arnold's sister

Arnold told her that he would have made the case that this was an educational field trip by a member of the departmental staff and could have sanctioned it as such.

With the passing years, as a result of his absences at home in London and in America, we saw considerably less of Arnold toward the end of his time in Leeds than we had in the past. However, when we were first married in 1961, it became our custom to give a dinner for a few friends each month and use these dinners to exercise our joint love of cooking and to try new recipes and dishes. I have kept the menus of many of these and I see, since we listed who the guests were on the backs of most of them, that Arnold was a frequent visitor to our first house at Weetwood Lane and then, just a few hundred yards away, when we moved to Weetwood Avenue.

In 1961, Arnold wrote to Ilse, 'Edward Allam (the deputy professor of music at Leeds) and I went to dinner with Margaret and Scotford at their new house. Delightful, delicious meal, both of them beaming and happy.'

I have the fondest memories of those dinners. Arnold had been told as a child that one should not 'couper le nez du fromage.' Because of this childhood admonition, he always did cut off the nose from the wedge of cheese at our dinner table – always asking permission first. Why did he remember that childhood rebuke in French, I wonder?

He would go into a reminiscent daydream over a particular dish, 'Ah, la daube Avignonaisse' he would say, 'and with a Côtes du Rhône,' and go on to explain how the recipe for this had been one of the sources of endless argument and debate as they lay, dirty and famished, in hiding in some cellar or attic in a safe-house somewhere in the Netherlands while they were ondergedoken, in hiding, during those war years.

On one occasion, Arnold remarked that he had never actually seen a toad close-up (we were talking about 'the toad, ugly and venomous, wears yet a precious jewel in his head' in a speech by Duke Orsino in *As You Like It*.) Toads are surprisingly territorial and I was able to get up from the dinner table, walk out through the French windows and collect the resident toad from a rose bed in the garden. I presented it to Arnold who sat there enthralled, admiring its famed jewel-like eyes with it in his cupped hands – where, first it inflated itself as a defensive signal and, when this didn't 'work,' it urinated into his hands. It was quickly returned to its place in the garden and our discussion then turned to *Macbeth* and the possible use of toad's urine in witch's spells.

Another curious feature of Arnold's visits to our house was the effect he had on our cats. He would arrive, enter, and the cats, who had spent the day in their customary feline idleness, would spring to life, race round the room, jump over the chairs, on occasion even climbing the curtains and generally 'putting on a show.' It was not some desperate attempt to get away from him, just simply wild behaviour for a few minutes on his arrival. They never did it for anyone else and he did not deliberately stir them into action – it was entirely of their own volition and they would soon calm down again. We never established a reason for this extraordinary behaviour but it was always a part of the 'occasion' of Arnold's visits.

But with the changing circumstances of his academic position, he spent less time in Leeds and his visits became less frequent. Margaret had retired from the university to permanent motherhood and we saw less of Arnold over the following years. Arnold was a happily married man, with a growing daughter on whom he doted, and his home, his real home, was in London.

6

LONDON

Arnold taught at Leeds University from 1956 until his retirement in 1976, with only those breaks when he gave a term of lectures at Pennsylvania State University, Cornell and Milwaukee in the United States. But Leeds was never his home. London was where he lived and where he was married to Ilse (née) Hellmann (1908-1998). At the time I knew them in London, they lived with their young daughter, Margaret (Maggie) in the tall, stucco, portico'd house in Drayton Gardens, Chelsea. I made several visits there when I had occasion to be in London and remember a house full of interest and curiosities, with the walls hung with pictures and framed prints and, inevitably, rooms lined with books. A fellow student from Devonshire Hall, who had been president there, Philip Sutcliffe, following graduation in dentistry, spent a year in London (1960-1961) and remembers the house as being a handsome family house and elegantly furnished. I do however remember that, as you walked up the stairs to go to bed, there was a series of Piranesi prints up the staircase – not what one would choose to look at on the way to bed with their wretched, tiny figures sitting despondently amongst overpowering ruins.

In London, Arnold took Philip round on those unforgettable walking lecture tours to the Temple Church (where they met Kenneth Clarke) and to the Westminster Banqueting Hall. And, while in Leeds, he and Philip visited Beverley Minster, one of the lesser-known Gothic marvels of east Yorkshire, a sort of mini-Westminster Abbey in the Wolds. Philip also drove Arnold to France to Normandy and then met up with him later in the Loire valley where they visited St. Savin sur Gartempe and also Notre Dame la Grande, both in the Poitiers area. The opportunity to be instructed by Arnold was one never to be missed and never to be forgotten.

Philip remembers collecting and delivering Arnold on these occasions as I also remember driving him to and from various places and appointments. Arnold said quite openly that he did not consider that he was of the temperament to learn to drive or to be a safe driver – a curious and, in its way, a courageous admission. While at Penn State, his inability to drive was a considerable shortcoming and his letters are full of the logistics of having to be collected or delivered to such-and-such place and being taken by willing friends to be shown the countryside and the places round the university. He even remarked that he might learn to drive while there and, in discussing by mail with Ilse, the possibility of the professorship, the acquisition of a car comes into the financial equations.

At Drayton Gardens, apart from her official psycho-analytical and psychiatric work, Ilse also had a private practice at home and saw patients there. Arnold had teasingly threatened to stroll through the room which she used as a waiting room, in a bathrobe and one of her hats – but of course never did so.

Among the more curious characters who came to Drayton Gardens was a handyman and joiner who, I think, 'came with the house.' His permanent job was as a diver with the Port of London Authority in the days when Chelsea was still a riverside working community and 'the diver' was allowed to have another job of occasional work when he was not required for his official tasks of going underwater to repair and maintain the structures along the river and its boats. This was still in the days of 'hard helmet' divers where they wore a domed brass helmet and lead soled boots. It was the household joke at Drayton Gardens that their handyman still wore his massive lead boots when he could be heard with a slow, ponderous heavy tread as he went about his tasks of repair and maintenance around the house.

Both Arnold and Ilse were immensely proud of and loving toward their daughter Margaret (Maggie) born in 1949 and she grew up in this high-powered intellectual hot-house and was as bright and self-assured, but well-mannered as you expect and hope such a child would be. She was treated as an adult by her parents and allowed to make her contribution to any discussion, being listened to intently and, one could not help thinking, on her mother's part, analytically.

Arnold had once remarked that, as a child, he realized that if he only spoke Dutch he would have only eight million people to talk to. Both Arnold and Ilse were fluent in at least half-a-dozen languages but they were afraid that, if they talked and mixed or changed their language as the topic or the mood suggested, their daughter would grow up speaking a multi-lingual macaronic of tongues, but none of them fully and properly. They therefore made the early decision that the house where Maggie was growing up under the care of her much loved nanny, Gretel (Mrs. Simpson), and their whole world should operate only in the English language. This decision appears to have been made even before Arnold and Ilse were married as Arnold's letters to Ilse from as early as 1947 are always written in faultless, idiomatic English with just, from time to time a phrase or part-sentence in German.

In this language decision, my Margaret, The Dragon, and I disagreed strongly with them since we were quite sure from personal knowledge and experience that, if 'at-home' had been multi-lingual, as soon as Maggie went to school, she would settle into English as her standard 'public' language irrespective of what was spoken within her family. In recent years, this has become a much more widely discussed topic as the children of recent immigrants have come into the public eye on television, in politics and elsewhere and have spoken openly about talking Punjabi,

Meijer, Arnold, Isle, and Margaret (Maggie) ca1951

or Polish across the kitchen table as children but going on to 'English' education and jobs without any problem, but with an enhanced understanding of language and how it works. Maggie was deprived of this advantage and only learned schoolgirl French at the Francis Holland School in Chelsea. There she developed a laid-back, drawling English which was quite distinctive, but she was also able perfectly to imitate her mother's heavy *Mittel-Europa* accent and even used it misleadingly to answer the telephone.

This lack of language exposure and proficiency on Maggie's part also led to one small, sad aspect of the Noach family life. Arnold's father, Meijer Noach spoke only Dutch and had survived the war in Holland. But when they met, he was never able to communicate directly with his young granddaughter who, of course, knew no Dutch. Maggie's daughter, Sophie later recalled her mother saying that the only word she ever remembered her father saying in Dutch was '*Godverdomme!*' when he cut himself while shaving.

Maggie did not go to university, instead choosing to work for several London publishers before setting up her own, extremely successful publishing agency, largely devoted to children's books. She was twice married and had a daughter, Sophie, born in 1989, by her second husband, the novelist Alan Williams. Unfortunately, Maggie had a back problem and died while undergoing remedial surgery for this in 2006 at the age of only 57.

Margaret Noach (Maggie) ca1969

When the Noachs settled in London in their own house at Wellington Square, Arnold acquired a dog, Bouncer, which was remembered with inherent dislike by all who met it. All of the family absolutely adored it. The dog was a sort of poodle-cross and had been bought, so friends said, from the high-security wing of Battersea Dogs' Home. The dog was good at heart and wanted to be loved by all, but Arnold saw no reason why this animal should be trained or disciplined in any way. As a result, it was a public menace to man and beast. When one considers Arnold's effect on our cats in Leeds, I now wonder whether it was something in his make-up which precipitated in Bouncer a similar, permanent, hyper-active condition. But Bouncer wanted to be liked and, if you sat as a guest on their sofa, it would come and look up at you with soulful eyes, put its chin on your thigh - and drool on you, copiously. More than once, I had to sponge down my trousers and send the suit to the cleaners as soon as I returned to Leeds.

Ruth Rosen describes being taken to meet the Noach family for the first time at Drayton Gardens and, as soon as the door was opened, this huge slavering animal throwing itself at her unrestrained. She is quite small and dislikes dogs and was dressed in a pretty, new dress and this totally unexpected assault upset her terribly for the whole of that first visit.

On its home territory, Bouncer could do no wrong. One visitor writes to me, 'Arnold was obsessed with (Bouncer's) "intelligence" - we were not so impressed! I remember an early visit to their house - 1958 or so - and we had a casserole for dinner at that lovely round table they had (at Wellington Square, before they moved to Drayton Gardens) Arnold served the food to about 8 of us (my neighbour was Veronica Wedgwood, the author), and ended up by giving the spoon to B to lick before putting it back in the casserole - none of us accepted the offer of second helpings!'

My friend continues, 'On another occasion (my wife) suffered an ectopic pregnancy while we were staying there and, following an emergency operation, spent a few days recuperating there. One day, while she was visiting the loo, Bouncer chose her bed as a suitable loo for himself - Arnold commented that it showed "how much he loved her"!

To take this dog for a walk around the tree-lined streets of Chelsea was a task for none but the most robust and physically strong. The dog, on a leash, would attempt to dash off in all directions, often simultaneously, so that it was constant tugging and lurching on your arm toward all points of the compass. Half-an-hour with Bouncer on a leash could result in muscle and joint damage to the arm which endured for weeks.

On one such evening, after an excellent dinner, delightful evening conversation and a penitential walk round the block with Bouncer, I retired to my room and was sitting up in bed reading. The room had a hand wash-basin and the bedroom door suddenly opened and Arnold came in with Bouncer. Arnold turned on the tap in the basin and Bouncer reared up on his hind feet and plunged his muzzle into the basin for a bedtime drink. Arnold appeared to see nothing wrong with this, but I made sure that I thoroughly cleaned the wash-basin myself the following morning before using it.

Bouncer at the basin

Throughout his working life, Arnold travelled extensively and frequently and his letters were written from many places particularly in Italy as he pursued his researches and revised work which had been on the go for decades. There are charming letters to Ilse, simply describing his activities, the places where he was and his general state of health, written as much by way of reports to her as simple descriptions. These continued from the 1950s right through to the 1970s. The last one which has been preserved was written from Venice on 4 September 1975. He writes to Ilse of time spent with mutual friends and his sheer pleasure in the city and the opportunities which its archives and its libraries afforded him.

Arnold and Ilse, Venice (1950s)

'Meanwhile I hardly ever stop feeling how lucky I am to be in Venice. Deselfde (sic – Dutch. *the same*) routine: 3-4 hours work a day (sometimes more when the spirit moves me) at the Fondazione Civi with its glorious library and phototheca on the more glorious island of San Giorgio Maggiore. Walks around the city looking at pictures, all in the service of Boschini. (Marco Boschini (1613-1678) Venetian painter and engraver). Muraro is an enormous help. (Michelangelo Muraro, director of the Venetian Ca' d'Oro museum and library). He is convinced that it will be a magnum opus, showing aspects far beyond anything so far done on the subject and he is happy as if he were my brother about my having broken my writing-block. This is incidentally as I see now only because Leeds is a heavy weight on my shoulders and I am glad it will be over by the end of next June (God willing). Among the centerweight(sic) or so of books, papers I have dragged with me for 1000miles is also the Ca' d'Oro catalogue which now, looking at it again, is something I am really pleased with. M. wants me to add little bits here and there to turn it into something for a wider public and not only the bloody scholars who are sharks anyway.'

Arnold did retire from Leeds University in June 1976, by which time had been awarded a personal chair and so became what he had always wanted to be, Professor Noach. His inaugural public lecture which all new professors are required to give, was a *tour de force*. He lectured on 'The Pillars of Hercules in Art.' He traced the theme and image of the twin pillars from classical Greece right through the whole history of western art to include everyone from the architects of the Greek and Roman temples, via painters such as Poussin and Claude Lorraine right through to the use of the twin pillar structure of Leeds University Parkinson Forecourt. It was Arnold at his best doing what he was best at – lecturing in public.

On 16 March 1976, Arnold was awarded the Knight of the

Order of the Lion of the Netherlands for services to the (Dutch) state and to art history. I believe that he received the actual award from the Dutch ambassador in London. A worthy recognition of all the work that he had done and the contribution he had made both to his own country and, indeed, to ours.

Arnold, Ilse, and Bouncer ca1970

In spring of 1976, while at home in London, he had suffered a heart attack which put him into hospital for a time and required that he followed, thereafter, a strict regime and diet. In his hospital room Arnold sat up in bed surrounded by banks of flowers from well-wishers, for flowers were still allowed in hospitals at that time, so that his room looked like a stand at the nearby Chelsea Flower Show.

He left hospital after a short period and returned home. A few weeks later, while preparing to go out for the evening, he collapsed. The doctor was immediately sent for and, apart from anything else, found that Arnold was severely malnourished. He had simply collapsed through being short of food. Arnold's response was that the doctor himself had prescribed the diet which he had been following. 'Good Heavens!' said the doctor. 'You don't mean to say that you've stuck to it? *Nobody* sticks to my diets! It's no wonder you're malnourished!'

Arnold made a recovery and quietly went about his business in and around his home in Chelsea. On 27 October 1976, he suffered another, fatal heart attack. He was only 66 years old and had lived a life of scholarship and connoisseurship and a life of great danger and hardship as well.

Some weeks later, a memorial reception was held at the house in Drayton Gardens. It was, as one would hope in memory of a man who radiated such cheerful bonhomie, quite a jolly occasion. Much of the social 'work' of the gathering was done by Maggie's first husband, a pleasant young American photographer and Jehovah's Witness called Andrew Delory. I only met him once and, on that occasion and found him charming and very good at that most delicate of jobs, being both welcoming and kindly and considerate to the guests who were all friends of Arnold's or of Ilse's and who needed to be handled with understanding and with care.

My engineering company had substantial continental markets and I travelled a lot on the commercial, negotiating side of our business. In Holland, I would use from time to time as an 'opener' the story of how I liked the Dutch since it was a Dutchman who had first introduced me to my wife. On an occasion many years later, I told this story and my client asked who that had been. I told him Arnold's name and he responded, 'Oh. You mean the man in the Resistance?' 'No,' I replied. 'I mean a small, jolly Dutch art historian.' 'Now you mention it,' he said, 'he was an art historian. But I know of him as a hero of the Resistance.' We knew that Arnold, while in hiding during the occupation, had 'done a bit with radio communication to Britain,' but to hear our family friend described as a 'hero of the Resistance' was astonishing and, quite simply, a shock to me. Margaret had found that his life was curiously compartmentalized and there were inexplicable gaps in his story, but it was this brief exchange in the offices of a Dutch company which served to inspire me to attempt this biography many years later. I only wish I had started on it much earlier when memories were fresher and more people were still around who remembered him.

7

LETTER TO ILSE
17 OCTOBER 1951

This hand written letter from Arnold to Ilse, from Amsterdam, again shows him going around Europe to try to reclaim his family funds from various sources. And his delight in his freedom to travel and his great pleasure in his wife and his daughter, Margaret (Maggie), now two years old.

Darling,

Bad luck: in bed with 'flu, getting better. I had a temperature <u>and</u> the doctor but I'm getting up tomorrow. Friday to Paris. I can hardly believe it. Wednesday or Thursday home, via Calais-Dover. I'll let you when exactly.

Touching letter but I am jolly glad you are feeling better. How is the back? I hope you'll look as well as you described yourself in your last letter. I hate pale faces. Pity my own is pale again. I looked and felt ten years younger at (?)Dicaw at

Kruitberg (Amsterdam) The house there is lovely. They take babies so I think we'll go there next spring. It is just the right place for you and Margaret.

Our affairs are in good order at last, after 6½ years haggling and conferring and letter writing. I also got a permit for the transfer of 70 pounds as a first instalment so that I can pay you back the arrears.

About Paris: I will stay at the Hôtel Recamier Place St. Sulpice or, to put it in a rebus:

Hotel  Place

Jetty and Ben stayed there last year. Quite good and cheap. I have only got fr.13.700, or 150 guilders in francs after a fearful struggle with the head of the (?)valute department of the Netherlands Bank, but I think it'll last 5 days for I'll take things in tins to eke out my life.

Poor little Margaret who is so sad. I'll never leave her again for such a long period. How did she get that protest against trousers into her head? Can't have been Ursula? I noticed the other day that she doesn't like her in trousers. Anyhow it sounds improbable that Margaret found it out and formulated her dislike for herself.

The dear old soul and her enquiries. [in German] For us [unreadable word] nothing more to be read.

It is unbelievable that in 48 hours I shall be in Paris. Would you let me know your friend's address at the hotel? I hope I still know my way about. Imagine I went wrong!

But no, that won't happen to
    Your faithful husband,

    Nol

8

ARNOLD

I have tried in the preceding pages, to write a coherent story of Arnold's life and career from his childhood in Amsterdam to his death in London sixty-six years later. I have, so far, deliberately eschewed analysis of his character or trying to describe the development and changes which his experiences had upon his mentality and upon patterns of his behaviour in later life when we knew him. But the nature of the life he had led, obviously affected him deeply and, in this chapter, I want to look into the changes which occurred throughout his life and how these manifested themselves in his later life and career.

Arnold was born in 1910 into a comfortable world in a stable and peaceful environment within a prosperous family. He was only four years old at the outbreak of the first world war and eight years old at its end so that, apart from a resented loss of some of his toys 'to give to the poor Belgian children,' little would have occurred to ruffle the tranquility of his upbringing. The form and passage of his childhood was almost pre-destined by the ambitions of his parents – his sister Julia to exploit her musical talent and to become a concert pianist, and Arnold to go to university and become a 'scholar of private means' – almost certainly as a university teacher or the like. And such was the path on which they both embarked and continued throughout the 1930s.

There was little drawback or dividing barrier in being Jewish in Holland. The Dutch Jewish population was mainly descended from Ashkenazi Jews but with a substantial proportion of Portuguese Sephardic Jews who had fled to the Netherlands as a haven after their expulsion from Portugal under Philip II of Spain in the seventeenth century. They had been an integral element in Dutch life, culture, and the arts for over four centuries, through until 1939. In Amsterdam itself, some 10% of the population was Jewish until the outbreak of World War Two and the beginning of deportations and the systematic murder of Jewish populations throughout continental Europe.

Under his former life, it was easy to be a non-observant and secular Jew and go right through one's life without one's ethnicity making a significant difference as to what one could or could not do and what one could or could not achieve. There was little anti-Semitism in Dutch culture before the rise of Nazi Germany in the 1930s whose wickedness and evil spread like a poisonous cloud across Europe, even penetrating into other countries where it had not previously been apparent. But in Holland it was believed that, as in World War One, the country could remain neutral and could to some extent offer a haven both to the Jewish populations of other European countries but also, to act as barrier to the turmoil which had swirled around the country as in the conflict of 1914-1918.

Obviously the international situation was a great worry, even in Holland and must have affected every aspect of daily life throughout the second half of the 1930s. The Blitzkrieg of May 1940 and the invasion of this previously peaceful country must have come as an appalling shock to all of Dutch society and more so to the population of some 150,000 Dutch Jews, together with those who had already recently sought refuge in the country from other continental countries, most particularly from Germany itself.

Arnold's previous life had been leisurely. He was not then, and was never thereafter a diligent or rapid worker. He could even be accused, not without reason, of being dilatory and, quite simply, lazy. From first entering the University of Amsterdam in 1928 until the acceptance of his doctoral thesis in 1937 was nine years – and that on a subject where all the required 'material' and relevant documentation was little more than a short walk from his home. But the choice of subject itself is of note and gives an interesting indication of the workings of Arnold's mind. He, Dutch, Jewish, the son of Miejer and Judith, chose to research and eventually to write the definitive history of the major Christian edifice of his country. And then, throughout the whole of his life, his scholarly interest was wholly in Christian architecture and art. Even when, two decades later, he came to Leeds, one of the major centres of Jewish history and culture in Britain, I never remember him showing any interest at all in the Jewish background and, indeed the architecture of the city.

At the time of his arrival in Leeds, there was an on-going *cause célèbre* concerning the fate of the Belgrave Street Great Synagogue, the original, oldest synagogue in the city. It had been built in 1860 but, as the city grew, its congregation had dwindled and moved out to the suburbs and the rather grand building with an adjoining caretaker's house, stood closed and derelict. The area was earmarked for redevelopment and the decision was finally made in 1983 to demolish it. But while it was still operational, Arnold was never heard to make any comment on it or on the very high level of Jewish cultural and social activity in the city.

Even in England, Arnold may have felt both the inherent

danger of being Jewish, from his recent experiences and also something of the shame of those who survived when so many others had perished. For many years, it was a subject not to be talked about and it is only fairly recently that those remaining memories have become general knowledge to the public at large. It is worthy of note that, even for those who survived the worst of the war and the concentration camps but were not Jewish, those who were to disappear into 'Night and Fog' like Floris Bakels, he did not put his experiences down into written record for thirty years after his liberation, while many more never spoke of it at all. Moreover, although inherently of Jewish background and culture in his original country, Arnold had been baptized in an attempt to avoid deportation and certain death under the Nazi occupation. As a ruse it was not successful and there must have been a degree of shame at this 'playing fast and loose' with one's former and one's assumed religion in order to save one's skin. It is certainly the case that others felt that way although, in any case, it was finally of no benefit.

Arnold came to London where he married Ilse in 1949. They lived at first in Wellington Square and Paul Hellmann remembers visiting them there where a characteristic of the household were Arnold's varying moods and humours. His mood was volatile and Paul relates how, on arrival, he would be 'tipped off' by one of the housekeepers, Mrs. Hipkins or Mrs. Martin, that they were having a hard time with him and that he was 'in one of his moods today.' This would soon pass however, though at other times he was known to explode into fits of temper which, fortunately, would soon go away and Arnold would return to his genial self in time for his glass of sherry before lunch or dinner.

The situation was not helped at this time by the fact that Ilse had been in the country for some years and had established herself with a 'proper job' and was, in effect, the breadwinner of the household, while Arnold was without regular employment or a means of making his financial contribution, an equivocal situation for a man at that time. In his letter to Ilse, written from Paris in 1951, he states, 'Our affairs are in good order at last, after 6½ years haggling and conferring and letter writing. I also got a permit for the transfer of 70 pounds as a first instalment so that I can pay you back the arrears.' However, Arnold's whole mood and behaviour was notably improved by his appointment as art history lecturer at Leeds in 1957. At last he was making a reliable contribution to the economy of the household.

From the time of his first arrival in England to his death thirty years later, Arnold wrote almost nothing – two short articles for *The Burlington Magazine* and a couple of brief monographs arising from his work at Windsor - that is all. Yet, in only two years, between 1937 and 1939, he had developed from his doctoral thesis a substantial book which is a well-written and presented work of close detail and which brings to architectural study a new approach of considering the architectural development of a single building, not only in terms of changes in building technology and style and the building's use and function, but of the extent to which those changes are influenced by the social and political changes that were taking place at the same time. Nowhere was this more apposite than in the Netherlands where, religious change, debate, imposition and the very nature of belief itself changed so greatly and impacted so heavily on every aspect of the life of the country and its people. The title which Arnold chose for his book '....*biography* of a building' tells us everything. This was a new approach and the book which he wrote became and remained for many years the most important work ever written on De Oude Kerk.

A few years later, coming to our shores 'because the food is better there,' Arnold never wrote anything substantial again. Just as it took Floris Bakels thirty years to put down on paper his terrible experiences of surviving war and concentration camps,

Arnold had been severely damaged by his experiences – of having to spend several years together when he knew that a single letter 'J' on a piece of paper could condemn him to a certain and terrible death, that unremitting stress for days, months and years together, of living 'rough' and being totally reliant as a supplicant and a vagrant on the courage, craft and kindness of other people – these took a toll on him from which he never recovered.

Three members of the Noach family survived the war in Holland. Extraordinarily, Meijer Noach had survived, as had his daughter Julia and his son Arnold. Given that more than 75 percent of the Jewish population of the Netherlands had been murdered during the Nazi occupation, the family situation was extraordinary. While Arnold was able to write to his sister in 1945 that, 'I feel alive again!' there must also have been a burden of guilt founded upon that eternal question among survivors, 'Why me?' It was, like all the other accumulated psychological problems which made up the burden of the survivors, a source almost of shame and hurt.

Many who knew him in England in the post war years will remember Arnold as a genial, cheerful, gregarious small man who was 'fun' to know. His formality shed with his jacket, he would roll around on the carpet playing 'bears' with my small son and read him bedtime stories with appropriate voices. He enjoyed good food and good wine and radiated a general air of 'bon vivant.' And within university hall circles, he would gather round him his Pickwickian young group and, in that younger entourage, he would talk, kindly, clearly and benignly 'like a Dutch uncle.'

But here was a man from whom a major function of his learning and his scholastic communication had been excised by the experiences of war. Those closest to him would have been aware. Others, less sensitive or simply less considerate, may not have realized. Arnold was war wounded, one of those *'mutilés de guerre'* for whom French public transport used to set aside special places on their trams, buses and trains. But it was not a conspicuous wound. He had not lost an arm or a leg or some other obvious evidential injury. But, nevertheless, he was damaged with little hope of full recovery and this manifested itself in the loss of his ability to sit down and put down on paper the accumulated experience of a lifetime of scholarship. He could 'talk it.' Even Quentin Bell had to admit, grudgingly, that he could 'deliver a good lecture.' Others recognized and were moved to mention this in the obituaries and encomia which appeared in the *Leeds University Review* and in *The Times* at his death. It is a sadder version of that obituarist's familiar phrase, 'he did not fulfil his early promise' but for very different reasons from those normally cited.

He remained a scholar and an extremely knowledgeable connoisseur of European architecture and art. His ability to communicate this verbally in the lecture hall was outstanding and anyone who was able to remember his predecessor, the unspeakably boring and lugubrious Arnold Hauser, will count themselves lucky that they studied under Arnold Noach and not under the previous 'Arnold.' In the field, he was even more charismatic and inspiring and would hurry off to indicate a point or an important detail or make a sweeping gesture to take in the whole baroque grandeur of 'Howard Castle.' And he was equally at home in almost any country across the whole of western Europe. His daughter, Maggie, once jokingly complained to him over dinner at Drayton Gardens, 'Do you know, Daddy, that I had been in every major cathedral in western Europe by the time I was ten?' Arnold kindly countered with, 'Oh, surely not, dear,' but Maggie was insistent - and she was probably right.

All this was lost by his untimely death. As professor Reg Brown had written only a few months before, on Arnold's retirement, in the *Leeds University Review*, 'One could speculate perhaps, casting one's thoughts back to those war years, on the nature of that evident block between mind and pen, which is so signally absent from communication by his lively and idiomatic speech.'

One can further conjecture that, had Arnold lived longer, say ten or twenty years, he might have found his way through the dam of his wartime experiences. From that last surviving letter written from Venice in 1975, he appears to have broken through into the ability to write again a 'magnum opus.' Quite how far he had got with it, we don't know. Today, none of his academic papers survive in the possession of his remaining family, so whether there were some notes, the structure, or a complete text of a work on Marco Boschini or a *catalogue raisonné* of the library of the Ca' d'Oro, they cannot now be found. But he felt in the autumn of 1975 that, at last he had recovered sufficiently that he would be able to produce a complete book again.

Unfortunately that opportunity did not arise and the whole of his accumulated art historical and architectural knowledge was lost at his death. We have only a single major work as a monument to his scholarship and, because, as he once joked himself, it is written in a language which 'only another eight million people can read,' his reputation and standing as a scholar and an expert are not what they should be as a result of his time and work in his adoptive country, England. This is particularly sad because, the opportunity existed to apply that original, analytical approach to the great churches and religious buildings of this country as well. Was there not the opportunity to research and write, 'York Minster, the Biography of a Building'? This would have been particularly fortuitous since in 1967 the whole structure of York Minster was subject to huge structural repair and renovation to stop it collapsing into the brick rubble remains of the Roman *principia* and the later foundations of the Norman cathedral upon which it had been built. The whole building and its structure and foundations were open to be seen. One of the most important religious buildings in northern Europe was laid open like the cadaver in Rembrandt's 'Dr. Nicolaes Tulp's anatomy lesson.' There was an opportunity which was there to be taken and could have been subjected to that original approach of analysis of the social and political implications of its architectural development down the centuries.

In that last letter from Venice, he says quite openly that Leeds is 'a heavy weight on my shoulders' but that it would 'soon be over next June.' However, we can clearly see from the outside that he would have been totally unsuitable to be the head of the fine art department and to handle the organization, the committee sitting and wheeler-dealing of funds and budgets that are a necessary function of the job of running a university department. And even more so a department which was to grow and develop in the range of its activities and the number of its students and staff. That Arnold was an outstanding scholar there is no doubt, but this did not make him a suitable candidate to be an administrative 'head.' Quentin Bell's successor, Lawrence Gowing produced the elegant 'solution' of a personal, emeritus professorship for Arnold and that was exactly right - a recognition of his status without the requirement to 'get his hands dirty' down in the detail of administration.

We also have to admit that Arnold could be 'difficult.' He was a paid-up member of life's Awkward Squad and it showed, not infrequently. He would vacillate when decisiveness was needed and be intransigent when compromise was required. He could also be 'prickly' and obtuse and needed handling with care and diplomacy. Administratively he was a problem. My future wife, Margaret Field, known for her 'Sir Humphrey'-like diplomatic skills, remembered the difficulties encountered with getting Arnold and the rest of the groups organized for those field study trips to Tuscany, Florence and even much nearer to 'Howard Castle.' It was, as we said in our family, 'like herding cats.' Even Arnold himself recognized that one particular habit would drive others to distraction. He always left arrival to get on a train, an æroplane or other public transport, not even to the last minute but to the last second. Strangely, I can never remember him actually missing a train, but his last minute dashes and leaping aboard were very bad for everyone else's nerves. He even recognized and admitted this problem himself. In his letter to Julia about his journey in summer 1945, he describes arriving 'after eight' to join a military transport which should have left earlier. Even then he picked up a lift to Nijmegen which finally left at 9.15 a.m. So typically Arnold.

He managed to have and to lead the type of post-war life to which he was best suited and which, to a substantial extent, he enjoyed. He created around himself a circle of friends and followers amongst whom he could be that father figure and 'Dutch uncle' and to some extent find himself back again among that younger 'set' whose company he had enjoyed in Amsterdam in the 1930s. He was also immensely proud of his wife and daughter and took huge pleasure in the day-to-day activities of his home and friends in London and all the things that there were to do in a capital city. He was essentially a city dweller and a flâneur of the city and where better to be so than in London and in Chelsea in the post-war period?

All of this probably enabled him to set aside the privations and the hardships which he suffered and, to an extent, to carry on where his life had so brutally been halted for the years of war, occupation and death. It is a source of sadness for all of us that his retirement and his further life should have been so suddenly cut short at no great age and with so much more that could have been said, done and, just possibly, written. In that last surviving letter of September 1975, he seemed finally to have broken through that 'block' which had inhibited him for three decades and to have written, or being able to write his 'magnum opus.' Sadly, we shall never know.

Arnold and Bouncer, London 1976

9

DE MORTUIS NIL NISI BONUM

Arnoldus Noach left a published legacy of only a single major work in the Dutch language and a few short articles in Dutch and English in scholarly periodicals. Looking at the books on my study shelves, there is not a single other spine embossed with that author's name, 'Arnoldus Noach.' Yet there should have been so many that were never written. On this, Professor Reg 'Spanish' Brown wrote in his appreciation of Arnold on his retirement from Leeds University in 1976, 'Not an abundant harvest from a mind so richly stocked and so generously opened to the enquirer.' Apart from that scant bibliography, we have nothing to go on except our memories of a man who reflected all the facets of someone whose life had been so seriously disrupted at just that time when he ought to have been able to settle in to the progress of academic life for which he was so obviously suited. But that was not to be. That critical period became, through no making or fault of his own, one of appalling upheaval, danger, fear and hardship and with the added risk arising from his 'doing a bit with radio communication to Britain.'

The man who was dispatched off to England in 1946 to recuperate was inevitably very different from what he might have been had he not experienced war, occupation and privation for five years in his own country. His first meetings and acquaintance with Ilse were certainly 'professional' for psycho-therapeutic purposes. Thereafter, apart from that major 'elephant in the room' of his permanent writer's block for the rest of his life, he had to recover a normality of living in a different country and permanently speaking a language different from that in which he had been brought up. He also had the task of establishing himself as an academic in art history, a subject which, at that time was, to some extent a newcomer to the world of formal, university learning in this country.

There was the Courtauld Institute established in 1932, and the Warburg Institute whose whole library, collections and the complete structure of the institute had been bodily removed from Hamburg to England in 1934, both since amalgamated and becoming a free-standing Schools within London University. At Birmingham University, there was the shell of a building with, in 1946, very little inside it. This was to become in time the Barber Institute of Fine Arts with its own beautifully designed and richly endowed art galleries and its own prestigious department of art history. And Oxford did not establish a free-standing department of art history until 1955. Art history had been a subject which you 'went abroad' to study and therefore the job opportunities in that new academic field were limited in Britain. It was for just that reason that Leeds University felt able to appoint as a suitable professor of fine art at Leeds, Quentin Bell who had no academic qualifications whatsoever, apart from having once been to school.

Into this world came a 'damaged,' foreign, Jewish, art historian, ex-resistance fighter who had been sent to England 'because the food is better there.' It is clear that Arnold was easily able to gain entry into Britain immediately after the war in recognition of his communication work with the Resistance and to be passed on to Ilse for remedial treatment. But he had to continue for some years in an equivocal position without permanent employment until he came to Leeds in 1956. Once there, he built a reputation as an extremely good lecturer and enjoyed that most rewarding, unofficial accolade of his lectures being attended by far more students than actually signed the attendance register. These were 'guests' from other disciplines and easily welcomed visitors who came because of his reputation and the fact that he communicated so well with his audience and that his lectures were of general intellectual interest. He was also invited, and acquitted himself extremely well, in giving lectures to the students of other departments where his knowledge of the art and architecture of a country was central to the study and understanding of its language and culture. Thus he gave lectures to the students of the departments of English, French, Spanish and Italian, all of which languages he spoke. He even lectured on the history of architecture to the department of civil engineering. He also acted as mentor and supervisor to numerous students and was, in short a very busy and effective member of the university department of fine art.

It is a great pity that, as a result of his untimely death, there is so little left as a documentary memorial to his academic and scholastic life. In part this must be attributed to the fragmentary nature of his work and of his life itself, compartmentalized and boxed in pieces and episodes with barriers between them.

It is very much more to be regretted that the situation was not helped by the head of the department of fine art at Leeds who had, with good reason, been appointed 'over his head' in 1959. Quentin Bell and Arnold Noach were of an age, both born in 1910. But what different lives they had led. Bell was born into that enclosed, bubble world of self-regarding, self-promoting 'superiority' which was the Bloomsbury group, who posed and navel-gazed (their own and each others') at Charleston in rural

Sussex where they painted insipid portraits (of each other, of course) and 'amusing' pastel squiggles on pieces of furniture and crockery and, indeed, on anything to which paint would stick.

Meanwhile, a Dutch scholar had been born and brought up in a country which had contrived to remain neutral in 1914-1918 and intended to do so again in 1939. Nazi Germany, the Blitzkrieg of 1940 and the aerial destruction of Rotterdam showed them otherwise. Arnold and his family did not choose war; they had it thrust upon them and had to live with its brutalities, its terrors and its privations for five years. Arnold was deeply affected by his war years and also by the experiences of his wife Ilse, who was steeped in the effects of the war on her charges and, at the end, by the dreadful revelation of the loss of so many members of her own nearest family in the Holocaust.

Arnold was 'damaged' and openly admitted as much to Quentin Bell from whom he received neither sympathy nor remedy. Bell writes of this at length in his 1990 work 'Elders and Betters.' He was appointed to Leeds to manage an expanding department of fine art. His art historian colleague had shown himself well capable of researching, presenting, writing up and producing a major work of art and architectural history, albeit in another language and in 1939, but I doubt whether Quentin Bell had attempted to read or even bothered to look into that volume. That Arnold was no longer able to write and was open about this, was a failure to be able any longer to give of his best. However, if you are a manager and find that situation prevailing in a colleague, it is your job, as a manager, to work out how to deal with it and get the best from him again. That is management. Although Arnold, at the end of his life, foresaw the way out of his writer's block by retiring from Leeds, he never again had the opportunity of recovering his former writing and literary skill. This was a severe failure – but it was also a management failure by Quentin Bell to do one of the jobs for which he had been appointed.

Had Bell recognized his own failure in that respect and admitted as much, it would have been excusable. The attitude which he took, however, was anything but. He sneered. This, in its way, is hardly surprising. The 'superiority sneer' was the default position of Bloomsbury. The whole of the Bloomsbury Group was a remarkable concatenation of arrogance, snobbery and anti-Semitism.

These attitudes pervaded his dealings with Arnold. In 'Elders and Betters' Bell consistently describes Arnold as his 'assistant.' He was, of course, nothing of the sort. He was a distinguished art historian and in academic terms, 'self-standing.' I find it astonishing that, in a work written in 1995, Quentin Bell could actually write of Arnold that, 'being a Jew, he would *probably have been unable to achieve anything* during the German occupation.' [my italics.] No, nothing except starvation, capture, transportation and death in a country where three in every four of his co-religionists were murdered. But Arnold had tried courageously to continue with his academic, art historical and lecturing work right up until his last public lecture on 18 April 1941 which was '*plotseling verhinderd.*'

He even had to suffer the humiliation of having to write that groveling letter in 1941 to some collaborationist bureaucrat in the Nazi controlled 'Department of Education, Science and Cultural Protection' asking if he might continue his studies and research at the University of Amsterdam despite the ordinance number 6. of 1941 (which forbad Jews to attend places – any places – of higher education). The reply was to be told to fill in the attached forms (in duplicate). We can guess that the first requirement would be to give one's official persoonbewijs number which, in Arnold's case, included that tell-tale 'J.' The outcome is not recorded but can be guessed. Within days of that event, Arnold 'ondergedoken' - dived under. He went into hiding.

Quentin Bell wrote 'Elders and Betters' in 1992, eighteen years after the first publication of Floris Bakels 'Nacht und Nebel' and two years after it was translated into English and published to considerable acclaim, in this country. Quentin Bell was able to write, apparently absolutely without irony that, 'the period 1939-45 was at Charleston a period of peace.' Did he never even look up into the sky and see his youngers and betters fighting to save his country or hear, at night, the roar of the bombers passing overhead?

During that 'period of peace' and down the years which followed, Bell was able to write a considerable number of published works, a great volume of writing, of which some three-quarters is about.....Bloomsbury and its posturing protagonists. Meanwhile, for years together, Arnold's life itself had hung, not on a book, not on an article, a sentence or a phrase but on the single letter 'J' on a piece of paper. Not an environment in which he could have been expected to 'achieve anything.'

I find the relationship between Arnold and Quentin Bell deeply regrettable. I found Quentin genial, affable and hospitable. Of course, as an engineer engaged in the dubious world of commerce and in attendance only as an appendage to my wife, Margaret, I was treated at Quentin Bell's various parties and other occasions with a certain condescension, but that was to be expected and was by no means unusual. As far as his position and his work as head of Leeds University department of fine art was concerned, he developed, expanded and grew the department and put it on a firm footing as a major part of the academic structure of the university. It is therefore a great pity that, in dealing with a significant problem with an immediate colleague, he failed. He not only failed, but did not even recognize it as a failure on his part except to pass over it with a Bloomsbury sneer and to trot it out in his autobiography as something by which to be entertained and amused.

The writing of an autobiography is itself, always suspect – it inevitably suggests that the author is endeavoring to excuse himself. You need to have the courage of Churchill to follow Benjamin Jowett's dictum, 'Never apologise, never explain.' But as Nigel Nicholson wrote in reviewing Quentin Bell's 'Elders and Betters,' '(the author) never suffers from discretion.' What the book does blatantly show however, is the author's lack of generosity of spirit. He gives a nod of approval to Eric Cameron but makes no mention of the brilliant originality of his 'process painting' abstracts which were developed while Eric was at Leeds. In the case of John Jones, whom he liked, he does not admit that John could show a clean pair of painterly heels to those who purported to paint at Charleston. Quentin Bell was professionally ungenerous and mean-minded. This extended to his attitude to Arnold's time at Pennsylvania State University, of which he writes dismissively, 'An American University asked him to come and teach for a term. He went, and they loved him. It seemed possible that he might return to them and they would give him that which he longed for – a Chair. American Chairs are more easily given than British Chairs and perhaps not quite the same thing, but he would at least be professor Noach. It seemed the happiest solution.'

It is indeed sad that there is little written memory of Arnold and that one of the larger records should be the belittling and deprecating sneers that Bell records in his autobiographical work. However, one can be consoled by the fact that his sneers were widely spread and nearly everyone gets spattered with the same dismissive contempt, which is audible above the steady roar of the torrent of name droppings which litter the work. Moreover, given that Quentin Bell writes of himself that he was 'not an art historian,' I detect in his systematic belittling of Arnold, who really did know and communicate his subject so excellently, a degree of professional jealousy – sneers and jealousy.

I have entitled this chapter, 'de mortuis nil nisi bonum (dicendum est).' Let nothing be said of the dead that is not good. My task and my duty has been to defend the reputation of a dear friend whose life deserves to be recorded and told. If, in order to do so, I have to transgress that dictum of Chilon of Sparta, I have to descend and to follow the example which Quentin Bell has already established.

Doctor Professor Arnold Noach, Knight of the Order of the Lion of the Netherlands, scholar, art historian, infinitely knowledgeable connoisseur of the whole of European art and architecture, polyglot, *bon vivant*, member of the Dutch Resistance, and kindly family man, deserves to have his story told, as fully as it can still be recalled. I remember him most importantly in my life as a loved personal friend and as the man who first introduced me to my wife Margaret, all those years ago and for that above all else I am and will remain eternally grateful to him.

10

EPILOGUE

In this short biography, I have tried to describe the life of my dear friend Arnold Noach and to analyse his character and his attitudes arising from the life which he had led, in peace and comfortable prosperity before World War Two, throughout the years of conflict, hiding and resistance, and then his recovery, marriage and family and his later, resumed academic life, with its difficulties and shortcomings, until his all too early death in 1976.

Assembling the information to do this has proved difficult. There is a paucity of first hand records remaining from the pre-war years (just a single surviving photograph of Arnold from pre-1939) and, understandably, it was a *sine qua non* of survival to leave no traces at all during the occupation and the *ondergedoken* years. Fortunately, immediately in the post-war years, Arnold met Ilse who was an inveterate keeper of letters. A substantial cache of Arnold's letters both to Ilse and, later on, to his daughter Margaret (Maggie) has been carefully preserved by

Sophie Williams, Arnold's grand-daughter. These have provided me with a remarkable insight into Arnold's recovery, his 'getting back together' and his roaming western Europe to reclaim his family's funds and to re-establish the mental structure of his encyclopædic knowledge of European art and architecture. It is these which have proved invaluable, with their mixture of sheer joy in freedom and being alive again, of rediscovering his old haunts and the small details of a daily life in which normality itself proved to be such a source of happiness and pleasure.

Arnold sculpted portrait, 1950s, attributed to Ismond Rosen

From all of this I have managed to assemble a coherent story of Arnold's life. In doing so, I have been fortunate in still having the help and generosity of a few key people who knew Arnold personally, and of having access to his letters and the family photographs from the post-war years. But one must add to this the fact that Arnold was a difficult man to know closely or in detail. As was found at the time of his retirement and his death so shortly afterwards, his life was curiously compartmentalized with barriers and gaps which frequently could not be filled in. Was this itself a manifestation of the carefulness and mistrust which came from those years 'on the run?' It is easy to believe that this was the case.

It remains such a pity that the person who actually had the opportunity to get Arnold fully to 'open up' and could have set him up to restart his original research and possibly his academic writing again – and would have been able, with care, to supervise and stand over him to make sure he did, should have failed to do so. Quentin Bell had that opportunity to 're-make' Arnold and kindly lead him through and beyond the 'writer's block' which had bedeviled him from the time of his first freedom. It is ironic that, at the last, Arnold came to see his position at Leeds as the on-going cause of this impediment and that retirement was going to be the solution. Unfortunately, we shall never know.

Personally, I am so very glad to have known him, because in the simplest terms, he was fun to know. From his delight in playing with our son, to the *bon vivant* air which he radiated and the pleasure of conversations and entertaining word-play, Arnold possessed a remarkable ability to 'make the occasion' and he records in his letters, the enjoyment which so many of these occasions afforded him as well. But, as I write this, I am two decades older than he was at the time of his death. How one could wish that there had been such a life-span for Arnold and what intellectual fruit might it not have borne? However, there remain many people, in Europe and in the United States who benefitted from his knowledge and his ability to 'give a good lecture' so we must, as we do in describing the public skills of speakers before the days of recorded speech, be grateful to have heard and to have taken in what he had to say on the multitude of art and architectural subjects with which he was so conversant. For those of us who had that privelage, we were indeed fortunate, and for those who did not have that opportunity, I hope this short memorial will serve to explain to them something of the *biografie van een vriend.*

THE AUTHOR

Scotford Lawrence is a writer, translator and art historian. He was a student at Leeds University in 1956, at the time when Arnold Noach came there and they first met in Devonshire Hall. Scotford spent his business career in engineering and, in retirement, took a further research and thesis degree in art history at the Barber Institute of Fine Arts at Birmingham University.

He is historical advisor to the National Cycle Museum in the UK and to two other museums in continental Europe and to private collectors.

He lives in Herefordshire in a village to the west of the Malvern Hills.

scotford.lawrence@care4free.net